Introduction

All you need to know about Inheritance Tax and Estate Planning has been written as a reference book to help give you advice. Inheritance Tax is payable on everything you have of value when you die. This includes your home, jewellery, savings and investments, works of art, cars, and any other properties or land, which includes any that are overseas. Karl and Tristan Hartey, experts in their field, both recognise the importance of addressing this matter and making sure you have all the correct policies in place to protect your estate.

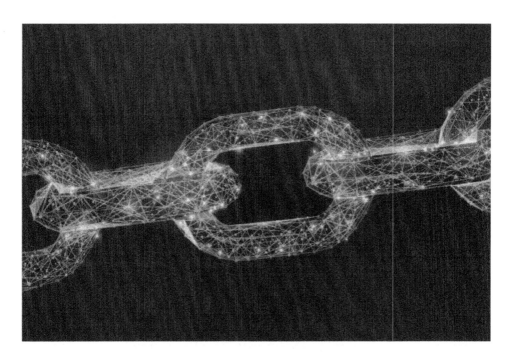

Chapter one
Inheritance tax overview

When we die, we like to imagine that we can pass on our assets to our loved ones so that they can benefit from them. In order for them to benefit fully from your assets, it is important to consider the impact of Inheritance Tax.

Inheritance Tax is payable on everything you have of value when you die. This includes your home, jewellery, savings and investments, works of art, cars, and any other properties or land, which includes any that are overseas. But there are certain circumstances if you put assets into certain types of trusts, for example, when Inheritance Tax becomes payable earlier.

Estate matters – what you need to know

When you die, your assets become known as your 'estate'. There is normally no Inheritance Tax to be paid if the value of your estate is below the Inheritance Tax nil-rate band (NRB) threshold of £325,000, or you leave everything to your spouse or registered civil partner, or you leave everything to an exempt beneficiary such as a charity. Unmarried partners, no matter how long standing, have no automatic rights under the Inheritance Tax rules.

Where your estate is left to someone other than a spouse or registered civil partner (for example, to a non-exempt beneficiary), Inheritance Tax will be payable on the amount that exceeds the NRB threshold. The NRB threshold has been frozen at £325,000 for tax years up to and including 2020/21.

If the value of your estate is above the NRB of £325,000, then the part of your estate that is above this threshold may be liable for tax at the rate of 40%.

Residence nil-rate band (RNRB)

The residence nil-rate band (RNRB), also known as the 'home allowance', was introduced in 2017 and now applies where the deceased owned a home, or share of a home, which is inherited by their direct descendants.

This also includes step-children, adopted children and foster children, but not nieces, nephews or siblings. Provided certain conditions are met, the home allowance gives you an additional allowance to be used to reduce the Inheritance Tax against your home.

Tapering away the value of your estate

The RNRB starts to be tapered away by £1 for every £2 if your estate is worth more than £2 million on death. Unlike the standard NRB, it's only available for transfers on death. It's normally available if you leave a residential property that you've occupied as your home outright to direct descendants.

It might also apply if you've sold your home or downsized from 8 July 2015 onwards. If spouses or registered civil partners don't use the RNRB on first death – even if this was before 6 April 2017 – there are transferability options on second death. The RNRB allowance is currently £150,000 (2019/20 tax year) and it will rise one more time to reach £175,000 in 2020/21 and in line with the Consumer Price Index thereafter.

Unused NRB on the death of a deceased spouse

If you are a widow or widower and your deceased spouse did not use their entire NRB, the NRB applicable at your death can be increased by the percentage of NRB unused on the death of your deceased spouse, provided your executors make the necessary elections within 2 years of your death.

To calculate the total amount of Inheritance Tax payable on your death, gifts made during your lifetime that are not exempt transfers must also be taken into account. Where the total amount of non-exempt gifts made within seven years of death plus the value of the element of your estate left to non-exempt beneficiaries exceeds the NRB threshold, Inheritance Tax is payable at 40% on the amount exceeding the threshold.

Reduced rate as a result of a charity bequest

If you leave something to charity in your will, then it won't count towards the total taxable value of your estate. You can also cut the Inheritance Tax rate on the rest of your estate from **40% to 36%**, if you leave at least **10%** of your 'net estate' to a charity.

Taper relief applies where tax, or additional tax, becomes payable on your death in respect of gifts made during your lifetime. The relief works on a sliding scale. The relief is given against the amount of tax you'd have to pay rather than the value of the gift itself. The value of the gift is set when it's given, not at the time of death.

Small gifts not subject to Inheritance Tax liability

HM Revenue & Customs (HMRC) permits you to make a number of small gifts each year without creating an Inheritance Tax liability. Each person has their own allowance, so the amount can be doubled if each spouse or registered civil partner uses their allowances.

You can also make larger gifts known as Potentially Exempt Transfers (PETs) and you could have to pay Inheritance Tax on their value if you die within seven years of making them.

Chargeable Lifetime Transfers (CLT)

Any other gifts made during your lifetime which do not qualify as a PET will immediately be chargeable to Inheritance Tax. These are called 'Chargeable Lifetime Transfers' (CLT) which could, for example, be a gift into a discretionary trust.

If you make a gift to someone but keep an interest in it, it becomes known as a 'Gift With Reservation' and will remain in your estate for Inheritance Tax purposes when you die.

Exempt transfers

HMRC lets you give the following as exempt transfers:

- Up to £3,000 each year as either one or a number of gifts. If you don't use it all up in one year, you can carry the remainder over to the next tax year. A tax year runs from 6 April one year to 5 April in the next year.
- Gifts of up to £250 to any number of other people – but not those who received all or part of the £3,000.
- Any amount from income that is given on a regular basis provided it doesn't reduce your standard of living. These are known as gifts made as 'normal expenditure out of income'
- Donations to charity, political parties, universities and certain other bodies recognised by the taxman (HM Revenue & Customs).
- Maintenance payments to spouses and ex-spouses, elderly or infirm dependant relatives, and children under 18 or in full-time education.

Setting up an appropriate trust could help

If you would like to make gifts to reduce a potential Inheritance Tax bill but are concerned about losing control of the money, setting up an appropriate trust could help. The rules changed in 2006, making some of them less tax-effective, as a small minority will require you to pay Inheritance Tax even before you have died. However, if appropriate, they can play an important part when planning for Inheritance Tax.

There are now three main types of trusts. Any number of different types of investments can be held in a trust, so it's essential to obtain financial advice to review your particular situation and requirements.

Bare (Absolute) trusts

With a bare trust, you name the beneficiaries at the outset, and these can't be changed. The assets, both income and capital, are immediately owned and can be taken by the beneficiary at age 18 (16 in Scotland).

Interest in possession trusts

With this type of trust, the beneficiaries have a right to all the income from the trust, but not necessarily the capital. Sometimes, a different beneficiary will get the capital – say, on the death of the income beneficiary. They're often set up under the terms of a Will to allow a spouse to benefit from the income during their lifetime, but with the capital being owned by their children. The capital is distributed on the remaining parent's death.

Discretionary trusts

Here, the trustees decide what happens to the income and capital throughout the lifetime of the trust and how it is paid out. There is usually a wide range of beneficiaries, but no specific beneficiary has the right to income from the trust.

A few trusts will now have to pay an Inheritance Tax charge when they are set up, at ten-yearly intervals and even when assets are distributed.

Proceeds paid outside of your estate

If you don't want to give away your assets while you're still alive, another option is to take out life cover, which can pay out an amount equal to your estimated Inheritance Tax liability on death. Ensure that the policy is written in an appropriate trust so that proceeds are paid outside of your estate.

Finally, one of the most important things not to neglect

You should review your Will if the value of your estate exceeds your NRB and you wish direct descendants to benefit from the RNRB. Making a Will is one of the most important things that you can do. The Government lays down strict guidelines on how money is to be paid out if you die without making a Will. By planning in advance, you can establish who you wish to benefit from your estate when you die, minimise any Inheritance Tax payable and reduce the risk of a dispute.

Inheritance Tax is a complicated area, and no one likes to think about their own mortality, so it is a subject that is easy to avoid. Making sure that you've made plans for after you're gone will give you peace of mind. With professional advice and appropriate planning, it can mean that you are safeguarding more of what is rightfully yours. Everyone's situation is different – to discuss your circumstances individually, please contact us.

Chapter two
Residence nil-rate band

The Inheritance Tax residence nil-rate band (RNRB) came into effect on 6 April 2017. The RNRB provides an additional nil-rate band where an individual dies on or after 6 April 2017, owning a residence which they leave to direct descendants.

During the 2019/2020 tax year, the maximum RNRB available is £150,000. This rises by a further £25,000 to £175,000 in 2020/2021, after which it will be indexed in line with the Consumer Prices Index. The RNRB is set against the taxable value of the deceased's estate – not just the value of the property. Unlike the existing nil-rate band (NRB), it doesn't apply to transfers made during an individual's lifetime.

For married couples and registered civil partners, any unused RNRB can be claimed by the surviving spouse's or registered civil partner's ersonal representatives to provide a reduction against their taxable estate.

Special provisions apply where an individual has downsized
Where an estate is valued at more than £2 million, the RNRB will be progressively reduced by £1 for every £2 that the value of the estate exceeds the threshold. Special provisions apply where an individual has downsized to a lower value property or no longer owns a home when they die.

For these purposes, direct descendants are lineal descendants of the deceased – children, grandchildren and any remoter descendants together with their spouses or registered civil partners, including their widow, widower or surviving registered civil partner – a step, adopted or fostered child of the deceased or a child to which the deceased was appointed as a guardian or a special guardian when the child was under 18.

Any unused allowance can't be offset against other assets

The amount of RNRB available to be set against an estate will be the lower of the value of the home, or share, that's inherited by direct descendants and the maximum RNRB available when the individual died. Where the value of the property is lower than the maximum RNRB, the unused allowance can't be offset against other assets in the estate but can be transferred to a deceased spouse or registered civil partner's estate when they die, having left a residence to their direct descendants.

A surviving spouse or registered civil partner's personal representatives may claim any unused RNRB available from the estate of the first spouse or registered civil partner to die. This is subject to the second death occurring on or after 6 April 2017 and the survivor passing a residence they own to their direct descendants. This can be any home they've lived in – there's no requirement for them to have owned or inherited it from their late spouse or civil partner.

RNRB is represented as a percentage of the maximum RNRB available

The facility to claim unused RNRB applies regardless of when the first death occurred – if this was before RNRB was introduced, then 100% of a deemed RNRB of £150,000 can be claimed, unless the value of the first spouse or registered civil partner's estate exceeded £2 million, and tapering of the RNRB applies.

The unused RNRB is represented as a percentage of the maximum RNRB that was available on first death – meaning the amount available against the survivor's estate will benefit from subsequent increases in the RNRB. The transferable RNRB is capped at 100% – claims for unused RNRB from more than one spouse or registered civil partner are possible but in total can't be more than 100% of the maximum available amount.

Personal representatives can elect which property should qualify

Under the RNRB provisions, direct descendants inherit a home that's left to them which becomes part of their estate. This could be under the provisions of the deceased's Will, under the rules of intestacy or by some other legal means as a result of the person's death – for example, under a deed of variation.

The RNRB applies to a property that's included in the deceased's estate and one in which they have lived in. It needn't be their main residence, and no minimum occupation period applies.

If an individual has owned more than one home, their personal representatives can elect which one should qualify for RNRB. The open market value of the property will be used less any liabilities secured against it, such as a mortgage. Where only a share of the home is left to direct descendants, the value and RNRB is apportioned.

Depending on the type of trust will determine whether the home is included

A home may already be held in trust when an individual dies or it may be transferred into trust upon their death. Whether the RNRB will be available in these circumstances will depend on the type of trust, as this will determine whether the home is included in the deceased's estate, and also whether direct descendants are treated as inheriting the property.

This is a complex area, and HM Revenue & Customs provides only general guidance, with a recommendation that a solicitor or trust specialist should be consulted to discuss whether the RNRB applies.

Limited by the value of other assets left to direct descendants
Estates that don't qualify for the full amount of RNRB may be entitled to an additional amount of RNRB – a downsizing addition if the following conditions apply: the deceased disposed of a former home and either downsized to a less valuable home or ceased to own a home on or after 8 July 2015; the former home would have qualified for the RNRB if it had been held until death; and at least some of the estate is inherited by direct descendants.

The downsizing addition will generally represent the amount of 'lost' RNRB that could have applied if the individual had died when they owned the more valuable property. However, it won't apply where the value of the replacement home they own when they die is worth more than the maximum available RNRB. It's also limited by the value of other assets left to direct descendants.

Planning techniques are available to address a potential IHT liability
The downsizing addition can also apply where an individual hasn't replaced a home they previously disposed of – provided they leave other assets to direct descendants on their death. The deceased's personal representatives must make a claim for the downsizing addition within two years of the end of the month in which the individual died. Different planning techniques are available to address a potential IHT liability, and these can be incorporated into the financial arrangements of any individual whose estate is likely to exceed the threshold.

Chapter three
Life-time transfers

Some people like to transfer some of their assets whilst they are alive – these are known as 'lifetime transfers'. Whilst we are all free to do this whenever we want, it is important to be aware of the potential implications of such gifts with regard to Inheritance Tax. The two main types are potentially exempt transfers (PETs) and chargeable lifetime transfers (CLTs).

PETs are lifetime gifts made directly to other individuals, which includes gifts to bare trusts. A similar lifetime gift made to most other types of trust is a CLT. These rules apply to non-exempt transfers: gifts to a spouse are exempt, so are not subject to IHT.

Survival for at least seven years ensures full exemption from IHT

Where a PET fails to satisfy the conditions to remain exempt – because the person who made the gift died within seven years – its value will form part of their estate. Survival for at least seven years, on the other hand, ensures full exemption from IHT. A CLT is not conditionally exempt from IHT. If it is covered by the nil-rate band and the transferor survives at least seven years, it will not attract a tax liability, but it could still impact on other chargeable transfers.

A CLT that exceeds the available nil-rate band when it is made results in a lifetime IHT liability. Failure to survive for seven years results in the value of the CLT being included in the estate. If the CLT is subject to further IHT on death, a credit is given for any lifetime IHT paid.

Transferred amounts less any IHT exemptions is 'notionally' returned to the estate

Following a gift to an individual or a bare trust (a basic trust in which the beneficiary has the absolute right to the capital and assets within the trust, as well as the income generated from these assets), there are two potential outcomes: survival for seven years or more, and death before then. The former results in the PET becoming fully exempt, and it no longer figures in the IHT assessment. In other cases, the amount transferred less any IHT exemptions is 'notionally' returned to the estate.

Anyone utilising PETs for tax mitigation purposes, therefore, should consider the consequences of failing to survive for seven years. Such an assessment will involve balancing the likelihood of surviving for seven years against the tax consequences of death within that period.

Determining whether taper relief can reduce the tax bill for the recipient of the PET

Failure to survive for the required seven-year period results in the full value of the PET transfer being notionally included within the estate; survival beyond then means nothing is included. It is taper relief which reduces the IHT liability (not the value transferred) on the failed

PET after its full value has been returned to the estate. The value of the PET itself is never tapered. The recipient of the failed PET is liable for the IHT due on the gift itself and benefits from any taper relief. The IHT due on the PET is deducted from the total IHT bill, and the estate is liable for the balance.

Lifetime transfers are dealt with in chronological order upon death; earlier transfers are dealt with in priority to later ones, all of which are considered before the death estate. If a lifetime transfer is subject to IHT because the nil-rate band is not sufficient to cover it, the next step is to determine whether taper relief can reduce the tax bill for the recipient of the PET.

Sliding scale dependant on the passage of time from giving the gift to death

The amount of IHT payable is not static over the seven years prior to death. Rather, it is reduced according to a sliding scale dependant on the passage of time from the giving of the gift to the individual's death.

No relief is available if death is within three years of the lifetime transfer. Survival for between three and seven years and taper relief at the following rates is available.

Timing of gift	Relief on the 40% IHT
Less than 3 years before death	No relief – full 40% IHT payable
3–4 years	20%
4–5 years	40%
5–6 years	60%
6–7 years	80%
7 years and above	Not liable to IHT

Tax treatment of CLTs has some similarities to PETs

The tax treatment of CLTs has some similarities to PETs but with a number of differences. When a CLT is made, it is assessed against the donor's nil-rate band. If there is an excess above the nil-rate band, it is taxed at 20% if the recipient pays the tax or 25% if the donor pays the tax.

The same seven-year rule that applies to PETs then applies. Failure to survive to the end of this period results in IHT becoming due on the CLT, payable by the recipient. The tax rate is the usual 40% on amounts in excess of the nil-rate band, but taper relief can reduce the tax bill, and credit is given for any lifetime tax paid.

Potentially increasing the IHT bill for those that fail to survive for long enough

The seven-year rules that apply to PETs and CLTs potentially increase the IHT bill for those that fail to survive for long enough after making a gift of capital. If IHT is due in respect of the failed PET in and of itself, it's payable by the recipient. If IHT is due in respect of a CLT on death, its payable by the trustees. Any remaining IHT is payable by the estate.

The potential IHT difference can be calculated and covered by a level or decreasing term assurance policy written in an appropriate trust for the benefit of whoever will be affected by the IHT liability and in order to keep the proceeds out of the settlor's IHT estate. Which is more suitable and the level of cover required will depend on the circumstances.

Covering the gradually declining tax liability that may fall on the gift recipient

If the PET or CLT is within the nil-rate band, taper relief will not apply. However, this does not mean that no cover is required. Death within seven years will result in the full value of the transfer being included in the estate, with the knock-on effect that other estate assets up to the value of the PET or CLT could suffer tax that they would have avoided had the donor survived for seven years. A seven-year level term policy could be the most appropriate type of policy in this situation. Any additional IHT is payable by the estate, so a trust for the benefit of the estate legatees will normally be required.

Where the PET or CLT will exceed the nil-rate band, the tapered IHT liability that will result from death after the PET or CLT was made can be estimated, and a special form of 'gift inter vivos' (a life assurance policy that provides a lump sum to cover the potential IHT liability that could arise if the donor of a gift dies within seven years of making the gift) is put in place (written in an appropriate trust) to cover the gradually declining tax liability that may fall on the recipient of the gift.

Level term policy written in an appropriate trust for estate legatees might be required
Trustees might want to use a life of another policy to cover a potential liability. Taper relief only applies to the tax: the full value of the gift is included within the estate, which in this situation will use up the nil-rate band that becomes available to the rest of the estate after seven years.

Therefore, the estate itself will also be liable to additional IHT on death within seven years, and depending on the circumstances, a separate level term policy written in an appropriate trust for the estate legatees might also be required. Where an IHT liability will continue after any PETs or CLTs have dropped out of account, whole of life cover written in an appropriate trust can also be considered.

Chapter four
Making a Will

If a person wants to be sure their wishes will be met after they die, then it's important to have a Will. A Will is the only way to make sure savings and possessions forming an estate go to the people and causes that the person cares about. Unmarried partners, including same-sex couples who don't have a registered civil partnership, have no right to inherit if there is no Will. One of the main reasons also for drawing up a Will is to mitigate a potential Inheritance Tax liability.

Where a person dies without making a Will, the distribution of their estate becomes subject to the statutory rules of intestacy (where the person resides also determines how their property is distributed upon their death, which includes any bank accounts, securities, property and other assets you own at the time of death), which can lead to some unexpected and unfortunate consequences.
The beneficiaries of the deceased person that they want to benefit from their estate may be disinherited or left with a substantially smaller proportion of the estate than intended. Making a Will is the only way for an individual to indicate whom they want to benefit from

their estate. Failure to take action could compromise the long-term financial security of the family.

What are the implications of dying without making a Will?

- Assets people expected to pass entirely to their spouse or registered civil partner may have to be shared with children
- An unmarried partner doesn't automatically inherit anything and may need to go to court to claim for a share of the deceased's assets
- A spouse or registered civil partner from whom a person is separated, but not divorced, still has rights to inherit from them
- Friends, charities and other organisations the person may have wanted to support will not receive anything
- If the deceased person has no close family, more distant relatives may inherit.
- If the deceased person has no surviving relatives at all, their property and possessions may go to the Crown.

Unmarried partners have no right to inherit under the intestacy rules

Without a Will, relatives who inherit under the law will usually be expected to be the executors (someone named in a Will, or appointed by the court, who is given the legal responsibility to take care of a deceased person's remaining financial obligations) of your estate. They might not be the best people to perform this role. Making a Will lets the person decide the people who should take on this task.

Where a Will has been made, it's important to regularly review it to take account of changing circumstances. Unmarried partners have no right to inherit under the intestacy rules, nor do step-children who haven't been legally adopted by their step-parent. Given today's complicated and changing family arrangements, Wills are often the only means of ensuring legacies for children of earlier relationships.

Simplifying the distribution of estates for a surviving spouse or registered civil partner

Changes to the intestacy rules covering England and Wales which became effective on 1 October 2014 are aimed at simplifying the distribution of an estate and could mean a surviving spouse or registered civil partner receives a larger inheritance than under the previous rules.

Making a Will is also the cornerstone for IHT and estate planning.

Before making a Will, a person needs to consider:

- Who will carry out the instructions in the Will (the executor/s)
- Nominate guardians to look after children if the person dies before they are aged 18
- Make sure people the person cares about are provided for
- What gifts are to be left for family and friends, and decide how much they should receive
- What provision should be taken to minimise any IHT that might be due on the person's death.

Preparing a Will

Before preparing a Will, a person needs to think about what possessions they are likely to have when they die, including properties, money, investments and even animals. Before an estate is distributed among beneficiaries, all debts and the funeral expenses must be paid. When a person has a joint bank account, the money passes automatically to the other account holder, and they can't leave it to someone else.

Estate assets may include:

- A home and any other properties owned
- Savings in bank and building
- society accounts
- Insurance, such as life assurance or an endowment policy
- Pension funds that include a lump sum payment on death
- National Savings, such as premium bonds
- Investments such as stocks and shares, investment trusts, Individual
- Savings Accounts
- Motor vehicles
- Jewellery, antiques and other
- personal belongings
- Furniture and household contents

Liabilities may include:

- Mortgage
- Credit card balance
- Bank overdraft
- Loans
- Equity release

Jointly owned property and possessions

Arranging to own property and other assets jointly can be a way of protecting a person's spouse or registered civil partner. For example, if someone has a joint bank account, their partner will continue to have access to the money they need for day-to-day living without having to wait for their affairs to be sorted out.

There are two ways that a person can own something jointly with someone else:

As tenants in common (called 'common owners' in Scotland)
Each person has their own distinct shares of the asset, which do not have to be equal. They can say in their Will who will inherit their share.

As joint tenants (called 'joint owners' in Scotland)
Individuals jointly own the asset so, if they die, the remaining owner(s) automatically inherits their share. A person cannot use their Will to leave their share to someone else.

Dying without a Will is not the only situation in which intestacy can occur
It can sometimes happen even when there is a Will, for example, when the Will is not valid, or when it is valid but the beneficiaries die before the testator (the person making the Will). Intestacy can also arise when there is a valid Will but some of the testator's (person who has made a Will or given a legacy) assets were not disposed of by the Will. This is called a 'partial intestacy'. Intestacy therefore arises in all cases where a deceased person has failed to dispose of some or all of his or her assets by Will, hence the need to review a Will when events change.

Chapter five
Trusts

Appropriate trusts can be used for minimising or mitigating Inheritance Tax estate taxes and can offer other benefits as part of an integrated and coordinated approach to managing wealth. A trust is a fiduciary arrangement that allows a third party, or trustee, to hold assets on behalf of a beneficiary or beneficiaries. Once the trust has been created, a person can use it to 'ring-fence' assets.

It is worth remembering that although the taxation of discretionary trusts is nothing new, generally the flexibility in the old regime meant that in many instances, where clients and financial advisers were planning inheritance tax (IHT) solutions, the potentially exempt transfer (PET) regime was simpler and potentially more cost-effective.

The relevant property regime that Interest in Possession (IIP) and Accumulation and Maintenance (A&M) trusts now find themselves in treats these trusts as similar to discretionary trusts for IHT purposes. The added complexities this brings does not mean IHT planning is no longer viable, it just means we need to look at the longer term view and really understand the objectives of our clients.

Trusts terms:
Settlor – the person setting up the trust.
Trustees – the people tasked with looking after the trust and paying out its assets.
Beneficiaries – the people who benefit from the assets held in trust.

Bare Trust

Simplest form of trust
They're also known as 'absolute' or 'fixed interest trusts', and there can be subtle differences. The settlor – the person creating the trust – makes a gift into the trust which is held for the benefit of a specified beneficiary. If the trust is for more than one beneficiary, each person's share of the trust fund must be specified. For lump sum investments, after allowing for any available annual exemptions, the balance of the gift is a potentially exempt transfer (PET) for IHT purposes.

As long as the settlor survives for seven years from the date of the gift, it falls outside their estate. The trust fund falls into the beneficiary's IHT estate from the date of the initial gift. With loan trusts, there isn't any initial gift – the trust is created with a loan instead. And with discounted gift plans, as long as the settlor is fully underwritten at the outset, the value of the initial gift is reduced by the value of the settlor's retained rights.

Normal expenditure out of income exemption
When family protection policies are set up in bare trusts, regular premiums are usually exempt transfers for IHT purposes. The normal expenditure out of income exemption often applies, as long as the

cost of the premiums can be covered out of the settlor's excess income in the same tax year, without affecting their normal standard of living.

Where this isn't possible, the annual exemption often covers some or all of the premiums. Any premiums that are non-exempt transfers into the trust are PETs. Special valuation rules apply when existing life policies are assigned into family trusts. The transfer of value for IHT purposes is treated as the greater of the open market value and the value of the premiums paid up to the date the policy is transferred into trust.

No ongoing IHT reporting requirements or further IHT implications

There's an adjustment to the premiums paid calculation for unit linked policies if the unit value has fallen since the premium was paid. The open market value is always used for term assurance policies that pay out only on death, even if the value of the premiums paid is greater.

With a bare trust, there are no ongoing IHT reporting requirements and no further IHT implications. With protection policies, this applies whether or not the policy can acquire a surrender value. Where the trust holds a lump sum investment, the tax on any income and gains usually falls on the beneficiaries. The most common exception is where a parent has made a gift into trust for their minor child or stepchild, where parental settlement rules apply to the Income Tax treatment.

Trustees look after the trust property for the known beneficiaries

Therefore, the trust administration is relatively straightforward even for lump sum investments. Where relevant, the trustees simply need to choose appropriate investments and review these regularly.

With a bare trust, the trustees look after the trust property for the known beneficiaries, who become absolutely entitled to it at age 18 (age 16 in Scotland). Once a gift is made or a protection trust set up, the beneficiaries can't be changed, and money can't be withheld from them beyond the age of entitlement. This aspect may make them inappropriate to many clients who'd prefer to retain a greater degree of control.

Securing the settlor's right to receive their fixed payments

With a loan trust, this means repaying any outstanding loan. With a discounted gift trust, it means securing the settlor's right to receive their fixed payments for the rest of their life. With protection policies in bare trusts, any policy proceeds that haven't been carved out for the life assured's benefit under a split trust must be paid to the trust beneficiary if they're an adult. Where the beneficiary is a minor, the trustees must use the trust fund for their benefit.

Difficulties can arise if it's discovered that a trust beneficiary has predeceased the life assured. In this case, the proceeds belong to the legatees of the deceased beneficiary's estate, which can leave the trustees with the task of tracing them. The fact that beneficiaries are absolutely entitled to the funds also means the trust offers no protection of the funds from third parties, for example, in the event of a beneficiary's divorce or bankruptcy.

Discretionary Trust Settled or relevant property

With a discretionary trust, the settlor makes a gift into trust, and the trustees hold the trust fund for a wide class of potential beneficiaries. This is known as 'settled' or 'relevant' property. For lump sum investments, the initial gift is a chargeable lifetime transfer (CLT) for IHT purposes. It's possible to use any available annual exemptions. If the total non-exempt amount gifted is greater than the settlor's available nil-rate band, there's an immediate IHT charge at the 20% lifetime rate – or effectively 25% if the settlor pays the tax.

The settlor's available nil-rate band is essentially the current nil-rate band less any CLTs they've made in the previous seven years. So in many cases where no other planning is in place, this will simply be the current nil-rate band, which is £325,000 up to 2020/2021. The residence nil-rate band isn't available to trusts or any lifetime gifting.

Special valuation rules for existing policies assigned into trust

Again, there's no initial gift when setting up a loan trust, and the initial gift is usually discounted when setting up a discounted gift plan. Where a cash gift exceeds the available nil-rate band, or an asset is gifted which exceeds 80% of the nil-rate band, the gift must be reported to HM Revenue and Customs (HMRC) on an IHT 100.

When family protection policies are set up in discretionary trusts, regular premiums are usually exempt transfers for IHT purposes. Any premiums that are non-exempt transfers into the trust will be CLTs. Special valuation rules for existing policies assigned into trust apply.

Value of the trust fund will be the open market value of the policy
As well as the potential for an immediate IHT charge on the creation of the trust, there are two other points at which IHT charges will apply. These are known as 'periodic charges' and 'exit charges'. Periodic charges apply at every ten-yearly anniversary of the creation of the trust. Exit charges may apply when funds leave the trust. The calculations can be complex but are a maximum of 6% of the value of the trust fund. In many cases, they'll be considerably less than this – in simple terms, the 6% is applied on the value in excess of the trust's available nil-rate band.

However, even where there is little or, in some circumstances, no tax to pay, the trustees still need to submit an IHT 100 to HMRC. Under current legislation, HMRC will do any calculations required on request. For a gift trust holding an investment bond, the value of the trust fund will be the open market value of the policy – normally its surrender value. For a loan trust, the value of the trust fund is the bond value less the amount of any outstanding loan still repayable on demand to the settlor.

Retained rights can be recalculated as if the settlor was ten years older
For discounted gift schemes, the value of the trust fund normally excludes the value of the settlor's retained rights – and in most cases, HMRC are willing to accept pragmatic valuations. For

example, where the settlor was fully underwritten at the outset, and is not terminally ill at a ten-yearly anniversary, any initial discount taking account of the value of the settlor's retained rights can be recalculated as if the settlor was ten years older than at the outset.

If a protection policy with no surrender value is held in a discretionary trust, there will usually be no periodic charges at each ten-yearly anniversary. However, a charge could apply if a claim has been paid out and the funds are still in the trust. In addition, if a life assured is in severe ill health around a ten-yearly anniversary, the policy could have an open market value close to the claim value. If so, this has to be taken into account when calculating any periodic charge.

Investing in life assurance investment bonds could avoid complications

Where discretionary trusts hold investments, the tax on income and gains can also be complex, particularly where income producing assets are used. The trustee rates of tax are currently 45% on interest and rent, 38.1% on dividends, and 20% on capital gains (2019/2020). Where appropriate, some of these complications could be avoided by an individual investing in life assurance investment bonds, as these are non-income producing assets and allow trustees to control the tax points on any chargeable event gains.

Bare trusts give the trustees discretion over who benefits and when. The trust deed will set out all the potential beneficiaries, and these usually include a wide range of family members, plus any other individuals the settlor has chosen. This gives the trustees a high degree of control over the funds. The settlor is often also a trustee to help ensure their wishes are considered during their lifetime.

Powers depend on the trust provisions, but usually include some degree of veto

In addition, the settlor can provide the trustees with a letter of wishes identifying who they'd like to benefit and when. The letter isn't legally binding but can give the trustees clear guidance, which can be amended if circumstances change. The settlor might also be able to appoint a protector, whose powers depend on the trust provisions, but usually include some degree of veto.

Family disputes are not uncommon, and many feel they'd prefer to pass funds down the generations when the beneficiaries are slightly older than age 18. A discretionary trust also provides greater protection from third parties, for example, in the event of a potential beneficiary's divorce or bankruptcy, although in recent years this has come under greater challenge.

Flexible Trusts with Default Beneficiaries
At least one named default beneficiary

These are similar to a fully discretionary trust, except that alongside a wide class of potential beneficiaries, there must be at least one named default beneficiary. Flexible trusts with default beneficiaries set up in the settlor's lifetime from 22 March 2006 onwards are treated in exactly the same way as discretionary trusts for IHT purposes. Different IHT rules apply to older trusts set up by 21 March 2006 that meet specified criteria and some Will trusts, but further discussion is outside the scope of this guide.

All post–21 March 2006 lifetime trusts of this type are taxed in the same way as fully discretionary trusts for IHT and Capital Gains Tax purposes. For Income Tax purposes, any income is payable to and taxable on the default beneficiary. However, this doesn't apply to even regular withdrawals from investment bonds, which are non-income producing assets. Bond withdrawals are capital payments, even though chargeable event gains are subject to Income Tax. As with bare trusts, the parental settlement rules apply if parents make gifts into trust for their minor children or stepchildren.

Trustees still have discretion over which of the default and potential beneficiaries When it comes to beneficiaries and control, there are no significant differences between fully discretionary trusts and this type of trust. There will be a wide range of potential beneficiaries. In addition, there will be one or more named default beneficiaries. Naming a default beneficiary is no more binding on the trustees than providing a letter of wishes setting out who the settlor would like to benefit from the trust fund.

The trustees still have discretion over which of the default and potential beneficiaries actually benefits and when. Some older flexible trusts limit the trustees' discretionary powers to within two years of the settlor's death, but this is no longer a common feature of this type of trust.

Split Trusts

Family protection policies

These trusts are often used for family protection policies with critical illness or terminal illness benefits in addition to life cover. Split trusts can be bare trusts, discretionary trusts, or flexible trusts with default beneficiaries. When using this type of trust, the settlor/life assured carves out the right to receive any critical illness or terminal illness benefit from the outset, so there aren't any gift with reservation issues. In the event of a claim, the provider normally pays any policy benefits to the trustees, who must then pay any carved-out entitlements to the life assured and use any other proceeds to benefit the trust beneficiaries.

If terminal illness benefit is carved out, this could result in the payment ending up back in the life assured's IHT estate before their death. A carved-out terminal illness benefit is treated as falling into their IHT estate once they meet the conditions for payment.

Trade-off between simplicity and the degree of control

Essentially, these types of trust offer a trade-off between simplicity and the degree of control available to the settlor and their chosen trustees. For most, control is the more significant aspect, especially where any lump sum gifts can stay within a settlor's available IHT nil-rate band. Keeping gifts within the nil-rate band and using non-income producing assets such as investment bonds can allow a settlor to create a trust with maximum control, no initial IHT charge and limited ongoing administrative or tax burdens.

In other cases, for example, grandparents funding for school fees, the bare trust may offer advantages. This is because tax will fall on the grandchildren, and most of the funds may be used up by the age of 18. The considerations are slightly different when considering family protection policies, where the settlor will often be dead when policy proceeds are paid out to beneficiaries.

A bare trust ensures the policy proceeds will be payable to one or more individuals, with no uncertainty about whether the trustees will follow the deceased's wishes. However, this can also mean that the only solution to a change in circumstances, such as divorce from the intended beneficiary, is to start again with a new policy. Settlors are often excluded from benefiting under discretionary and flexible trusts. Where this applies, this type of trust isn't suitable for use with joint life, first death protection policies if the primary purpose is for the proceeds to go to the survivor.

Chapter six
Lasting power of attorney

A lasting power of attorney (LPA) enables individuals to take control of decisions that affect them, even in the event that they can't make those decisions for themselves. Without them, loved ones could be forced to endure a costly and lengthy process to obtain authority to act for an individual who has lost mental capacity.

An individual can create an LPA covering their property and financial affairs and/or a separate LPA for their health and welfare. It's possible to appoint the same or different attorneys in respect of each LPA, and both versions contain safeguards against possible misuse.

Individual loses the capacity to manage their own financial affairs
It's not hard to imagine the difficulties that could arise where an individual loses the capacity to manage their own financial affairs and

without access to their bank account, pension and investments, family and friends could face an additional burden at an already stressful time. LPAs and their equivalents in Scotland and Northern Ireland should be a consideration in all financial planning discussions and should be a key part of any protection insurance planning exercise. Planning for mental or physical incapacity should sit alongside any planning for ill health or unexpected death.

Commencing from 1 October 2007, it is no longer possible to establish a new Enduring Power of Attorney EPA in England and Wales, but those already in existence remain valid. The attorney would have been given authority to act in respect of the donor's property and financial affairs as soon as the EPA was created. At the point the attorney believes the donor is losing their mental capacity, they would apply to the Office of the Public Guardian (OPG) to register the EPA to obtain continuing authority to act.

Giving authority to a chosen attorney in respect of financial and property matters
Similar provisions to LPAs apply in Scotland. The 'granter' (donor) gives authority to their chosen attorney in respect of their financial and property matters ('continuing power of attorney') and/or personal welfare ('welfare power of attorney'). The latter only takes effect upon the granter's mental incapacity. Applications for powers of attorney must be accompanied by a certificate confirming the granter understands what they are doing, completed by a solicitor or medical practitioner only.

LPAs don't apply to Northern Ireland. Instead, those seeking to make a power of appointment over their financial affairs would complete an EPA. This would be effective as soon as it was completed and would only need to be registered in the event of the donor's loss of mental capacity with the High Court (Office of Care and Protection).

Where the donor has lost mental capacity in the opinion of a medical practitioner
It's usual for the attorney to be able to make decisions about the donor's financial affairs as soon as the LPA is registered.

Alternatively, the donor can state it will only apply where the donor has lost mental capacity in the opinion of a medical practitioner.

An LPA for health and welfare covers decisions relating to an individual's day-to-day well-being. The attorney may only act once the donor lacks mental capacity to make the decision in question. The types of decisions covered might include where the donor lives and decisions concerning medical treatment.

Option to provide authority to give or refuse consent for life-sustaining treatment
The donor also has the option to provide their attorney with the authority to give or refuse consent for life sustaining treatment. Where no authority is given, treatment will be provided to the donor in their best interests. Unlike the registration process for an EPA, registration for both types of LPA takes place up front and is not dependent on the donor's mental capacity.

An attorney must act in the best interest of the donor, following any instructions and considering the donor's preferences when making decisions.

They must follow the Mental Capacity Act Code of Practice which establishes five key principles:

1. A person must be assumed to have capacity unless it's established he or she lacks capacity.
2. A person isn't to be treated as unable to make a decision unless all practicable steps to help him or her do so have been taken without success.
3. A person isn't to be treated as unable to make a decision merely because he or she makes an unwise decision.
4. An act done, or decision made, under the Act for or on behalf of a person who lacks capacity must be done, or made, in his or her best interests.
5. Before the act is done, or the decision is made, regard must be had to whether the purpose for which it's needed can be as effectively achieved in a way that is less restrictive of the person's rights and freedom of action.

Trust corporation can be an attorney for a property and financial affairs LPA

A donor with mild dementia might be provided with the means to purchase items for daily living, but otherwise their financial matters are undertaken by their attorney. The code of practice applies a number of legally binding duties upon attorneys, including the requirement to keep the donor's money and property separate from their own or anyone else's.

Anyone aged 18 or over who has mental capacity and isn't an undischarged bankrupt may act as an attorney. A trust corporation can be an attorney for a property and financial affairs LPA. In practice, attorneys will be spouses, family members or friends, or otherwise professional contacts such as solicitors.

Relating to things an attorney should or shouldn't do when making decisions

Where joint attorneys are being appointed, the donor will state whether they act jointly (the attorneys must make all decisions together), or jointly and severally (the attorneys may make joint decisions or separately), or jointly for some decisions (for example, the sale of the donor's property) and jointly and severally in respect of all other decisions. An optional but useful feature of the LPA is the ability to appoint a replacement attorney in the event the original attorney is no longer able to act.

The donor can leave instructions and preferences, but if they don't their attorney will be free to make any decisions they feel are correct. Instructions relate to things the attorney should or shouldn't do when making decisions – not selling the donor's home, unless a doctor states the donor can no longer live independently or a particular dietary requirement would be examples.

Beliefs and values an attorney has to consider when acting on the donor's behalf

Preferences relate to the donor's wishes, beliefs and values they would like their attorney to consider when acting on their behalf.

Examples might be ethical investing or living within close proximity of a relative.

The following apply to both forms of LPA. A 'certificate provider' must complete a section in the LPA form stating that as far as they are aware, the donor has understood the purpose and scope of the LPA. A certificate provider will be an individual aged 18 or over and either, someone who has known the donor personally well for at least two years; or someone chosen by the donor on account of their professional skills and expertise – for example, a GP or solicitor.

Allowing for any concerns or objections to be raised before the LPA is registered
There are restrictions on who may act as a certificate provider – these include attorneys, replacement attorneys, family members and business associates of the donor. A further safeguard is the option for the donor to choose up to five people to be notified when an application for the LPA to be registered is being made.

This allows any concerns or objections to be raised before the LPA is registered which must be done within five weeks from the date on which notice is given. The requirement to obtain a second certificate provider where the donor doesn't include anyone to be notified has now been removed as part of the Office of the Public Guardian (OPG) review of LPAs.

Strict limits on the type of gifts attorneys can make on the donor's behalf
A person making an LPA can have help completing it, but they must have mental capacity when they fill in the forms. Otherwise, those seeking to make decisions on their behalf will need to apply to the Court of Protection for a deputyship order. This can be expensive and time-consuming and may require the deputy to submit annual reports detailing the decisions they have made.

There are strict limits on the type of gifts attorneys can make on the donor's behalf. Gifts may be made on 'customary occasions', for example, birthdays, marriages and religious holidays, or to any charity to which the donor was accustomed to donating. Gifts falling outside of these criteria would need to be approved by the Court of Protection. An example would be a gift intended to reduce the donor's Inheritance Tax liability.

Chapter seven
Wealth preservation

Whether you have earned your wealth, inherited it or made shrewd investments, you will want to ensure that as little of it as possible ends up in the hands of HM Revenue & Customs. With careful planning and professional financial advice, it is possible to take preventative action to either reduce or mitigate a persons beneficiaries' Inheritance Tax (IHT) bill – or mitigate it altogether. These are some of the main areas to consider.

1. Make a Will
A vital element of effective estate preservation is to make a Will. According to the Law Commission (England and Wales), nearly 60%of UK adults don't have a Will. This is mainly due to apathy but

also a result of the fact that many people feel uncomfortable talking about issues surrounding death. Making a Will ensures an individual's assets are distributed in accordance with their wishes. This is particularly important if the person has a spouse or registered civil partner. Even though there is no Inheritance Tax payable between both parties, there could be tax payable if one person dies intestate without a Will.

Without a Will in place, an estate falls under the laws of intestacy – and this means the estate may not be divided up in the way the deceased person wanted it to be.

2. Make allowable gifts
A person can give cash or gifts worth up to £3,000 in total each tax year, and these will be exempt from Inheritance Tax when they die. They can carry forward any unused part of the £3,000 exemption to the following year, but they must use it or it will be lost.

Small gifts of up to £250 a year can also be made to as many people as an individual likes.

3. Give away assets
Parents are increasingly providing children with funds to help them buy their own home. This can be done through a gift, and provided the parents survive for seven years after making it, the money automatically moves outside of their estate for IHT calculations, irrespective of size.

4. Make use of trusts
Assets can be put in an appropriate trust, thereby no longer forming part of the estate. There are many types of trust available and can be set up simply at little or no charge. They usually involve parents (settlors) investing a sum of money into a trust. The trust has to be set up with trustees – a suggested minimum of two – whose role is to ensure that on the death of the settlers, the investment is paid out according to the settlors' wishes. In most cases, this will be to children or grandchildren.

The most widely used trust is a discretionary trust and can be set up in a way that the settlors (parents) still have access to income or parts of the capital. It can seem daunting to put money away in a trust, but they can be unwound in the event of a family crisis and monies returned to the settlors via the beneficiaries.

5. The income over expenditure rule
As well as putting lump sums into an appropriate trust, people can also make monthly contributions into certain savings or insurance policies and put them into an appropriate trust. The monthly contributions are potentially subject to IHT, but if the person can prove that these payments are not compromising their standard of living, they are exempt.

6. Provide for the tax
If a person is not in a position to take avoiding action, an alternative approach is to make provision for paying IHT when it is due. The tax has to be paid within six months of death (interest is added after this time). Because probate must be granted before any money can be released from an estate, the executor may have to borrow money or use their own funds to pay the IHT bill.

This is where life assurance policies written in an appropriate trust come into their own. A life assurance policy is taken out on both a husband's and wife's life with the proceeds payable only on second death. The amount of cover should be equal to the expected Inheritance Tax liability. By putting the policy in an appropriate trust, it means it does not form part of the estate.

The proceeds can then be used to pay any IHT bill straightaway without the need for the executors to borrow.

Chapter eight
Pension & IHT planning

The Government has introduced comprehensive reforms to the pension rules over the previous few years. One important change, which may have been overlooked by some savers, is the reduction of the Lifetime Allowance that applies to pension savings. This further reduction means that you may be affected.

Pension planning and making contributions for others can be an effective way for the donor to reduce their taxable estate while saving into a pension for someone else.

- Pension contributions for others can be an effective way for the donor to reduce their taxable estate while saving into a pension for someone else.
- Pensions are exempt from paying Inheritance Tax and can be passed down to the next generation.

- It is good planning using up assets subject to inheritance tax before using pension assets.
- Spousal bypass trusts were very popular before pension flexibility, to avoid inheritance tax on a quick second death. However, spousal bypass trusts are still useful in certain circumstances.

Many inheritance tax (IHT) planning strategies involve making significant capital payments. The objective in doing so is to reduce the taxable estate. A trust is often used to retain control over the ultimate destination and timing of benefits.

PENSION ARE A LONG-TERM INVESTMENT. THE FUND VALUE MAY FLUCTUATE AND CAN GO DOWN, WHICH WOULD HAVE AN IMPACT ON THE LEVEL OF PENSION BENEFITS AVAILABLE.

YOUR PENSION INCOME COULD ALSO BE AFFECTED BY INTEREST RATES AT THE TIME YOU TAKE YOUR BENEFITS. THE TAX IMPLICATIONS OF PENSION WITHDRAWALS WILL BE BASED ON YOUR INDIVIDUAL CIRCUMSTANCES, TAX LEGISLATION AND REGULATION, WHICH ARE SUBJECT TO CHANGE IN THE FUTURE.

Chapter nine
Later life care

Have you thought about the cost of care in later life? One of the biggest challenges of the 21st century is Britain's ageing population. There is continually much talk about later life care in the media, and it's a subject that is going to be one of the biggest social challenges in the coming years.

As later life care becomes more prevalent, whether you are considering this for yourself or a relative, the challenge of covering the costs involved can be significant. In addition, the options for funding later life care are fiendishly complex.

Complex, sensitive set of challenges
Looking after the care needs and financial affairs of your loved ones as they grow older presents a complex, sensitive set of challenges. Under the changes proposed in the Care Act 2014, which received the Royal Assent in May 2014 and which came into effect in April 2016, the funding of elderly care changed significantly.

One of the perceived benefits under the new system is that eligible care costs are to be subject to a lifetime cap from 2020. This is not as beneficial as it may seem, however, because the cap does not include the 'board and lodging' element of the care costs, which currently normally exceeds £1,000 per month. Furthermore, the legislation provides that these costs may be varied in line with average earnings.

Destroying any hopes of passing wealth
Within a matter of only a few years, a family's assets built up over generations can disappear in the payment of care home fees. Choosing the wrong approach can bleed families dry financially, destroying any hopes of passing wealth on to the next generation. Increasingly, those in the sandwich generation (a generation of people who care for their ageing parents whilst supporting their own children) also need to be considerate of their future needs, the costs and not becoming a burden on their own children.

Later life care is a very broad term, covering everything from temporary placements for those who need to recuperate from a fall or illness, to round-the-clock dementia care and end-of-life palliative care. You or a family member may need different types of care at different times in life, so it is important to build in flexibility to meet changing needs.

Financial picture and approach can change
Depending on what type of care is needed, the financial picture and approach can change. Someforms of benefit are only available to those with very severe medical needs, while different rules apply when care is likely to be temporary rather than permanent. There are also some forms of care available at home, which can be a less costly alternative to full residential care, depending on the needs of the individual, while warden-controlled or sheltered housing can also be an option.

First step towards getting help and support
A local authority care assessment – or social care assessment – from your local council is a good place to start, particularly if you

are confused about a relative's needs, and is essential if you are hoping that the council will fund any part of their care. It can also be the first step towards getting the help and support needed for everyday life.

The council has a statutory duty to provide this, and it should be carried out by a qualified health professional. The aim of a care needs assessment is to work out how much help is needed. After it is completed, a care plan will provide advice detailing what type of care is appropriate, and they'll carry out a financial assessment. This is called a 'means test'. This will work out if you need to contribute towards the cost of care, and whether the local authority will pay for all or some of the care costs.

Financial support from the local authority
It is a common misconception that gifting away a property will mean it cannot be taken into account as an asset for assessing care costs if the time between the gift and the need to go into care is significant. This is not strictly the case. However, a property occupied by a dependent over the age of 60 cannot be counted as an asset for this purpose. If you have a relative that lives in England or Northern Ireland and they've been assessed as needing a care home place and their capital is below £23,250 (or in Scotland £26,500 and Wales £30,000), they should be entitled to financial support from the local authority. In England or Northern Ireland, a proportion of the cost is paid until the capital falls to £14,250, but this is different in Scotland and Wales.

Requiring nursing care or other specific care
Not all types of care home are suitable for all needs. If your relative needs nursing care, for example, they will need a home that offers more support than an ordinary care home. For those requiring nursing care or other specific care, the bill is higher, while some people may wish to choose more expensive care homes for their relatives because they prefer the facilities or the ambience.

If you do this, you need to ensure your relative will have sufficient money to stay there for a potentially long period of time, or that your family is able to pay any proportion of the bill that is not being met by the local authority.

When planning for later life care needs, think about:

- Who (in your family) most needs care and for how long

- Whether you need a care plan now

- Whether you should be planning ahead for yourself, a loved one or other relative

- Whether you have the money to pay for care

- How long you might need to pay for a care plan

- Whether home care or a nursing home is required

- What kinds of things would be required of the help, for example, help with dressing, using the toilet, feeding or mobility.

- Whether you find that your home requires additional features such as a stair lift, an opening and closing bath or a bath chair, and/or home help.

How to fund the cost of care provision in later life

We are all likely to live longer and healthier lives than past generations but with the added challenge of how to ensure we have adequate resources to allow us to live the life that we would like in those later years. Understandably, the problem this subject poses is how to fund the cost of care provision in later life, which can be very worrying for many families.

We understand that making plans for your later years – or an elderly parent's - is a sensitive and emotional process. There is the uncertainty of not knowing whether you will need some form of care in the future and, if so, to what extent. And, of course, you'll need to know the financial implications.

Chapter ten
Long-term care

It's a concern for many people how they will pay the cost of care either for themselves or for a loved one. The reality is that most people will be expected to pay something towards these costs. With the UK's population ageing, more people will be living with long-term care needs.

As we get older, it becomes more likely that we may need day-to-day help with activities such as washing and dressing, or help with household activities such as cleaning and cooking.

A good life in old age
Not only is the demand for long-term care expected to rise thanks in part to our ageing population, but also due to an increasing prevalence of conditions such as dementia. This makes planning ahead essential, but when it comes to funding later life it can get quite

complicated, particularly since the costs depend on several unknowns, including how long we are going to live.

The matter is further exacerbated because of how local authorities calculate whether a person needs financial assistance for the cost of residential care.

The average cost of a care home place in the UK is £30,000 a year, and £40,000 if nursing care is required; if you live in the South East of England, the price is likely to be more, according to The Money Advice Service. Even if you're going down the care-at-home route, you'll find that at approximately £17 an hour, two hours of daily care could amount to almost £12,500 a year.

Level of state support
The level of state support received can be different depending on whether you live in England, Wales, Scotland or Northern Ireland.

In England and Wales, for example, currently you can receive means-tested state assistance, which depends on your savings and assets. For instance, if your savings and assets are above £23,250 (England) or £30,000 (Wales), you will normally be expected to pay for the full cost of long-term care yourself.
Government state benefits can also provide some help but may not be enough or may not pay for the full cost of long-term care.

Financial support assitance
Long-term care insurance can provide the financial support you need if you have to pay for care assistance for yourself or a loved one.
Additionally, some long-term care insurance will cover the cost of assistance for those who need help to perform the basic activities of daily life such as getting out of bed, dressing, washing and going to the toilet.

You can receive long-term care in your own home or in residential or nursing homes.

Regardless of where you receive care, paying for care in old age is a growing issue.

Planning for long-term care
There are a number of different ways to fund long-term care. These are some of the main options available for people needing to make provision.

Immediate needs annuities
This annuity is a type of insurance policy that provides a regular income in exchange for an upfront lump sum investment. When used for long-term care, it provides a guaranteed income for life to pay for care costs in exchange for a one-off lump sum payment if you have care needs now. Income is tax-free if it is paid directly to the care provider.

Enhanced Annuities
You can use your pension to purchase an enhanced annuity (also known as an 'impaired life annuity') if you have a health problem, a long-term illness, if you are overweight or if you smoke. Annuity providers use full medical underwriting to determine a more accurate individual price. People with medical conditions including Parkinson's disease and multiple sclerosis, or those who have had a major organ transplant, are likely to be eligible for an enhanced annuity.

Equity release schemes
If you need to fund your long-term care and have already paid off (or nearly paid off) your mortgage, an equity release scheme could be one option to consider if appropriate. It is important to obtain professional financial advice before committing to an equity release scheme. Your individual circumstances need to be assessed, and this is why financial advice is a must in the process and a regulatory requirement.

These schemes give you the ability to obtain a cash lump sum as a loan secured on your home. However, it's essential to make an informed decision and consider the options and alternatives available and any implications regarding state benefits, local authority support and tax obligations.

Savings and investments
These two methods enable you to plan ahead and ensure your savings and assets are in place for your future care needs.

If you are already retired, or nearing retirement, you should ensure that your financial affairs are in order – for example, arranging or updating your Will or a Power of Attorney. It also makes sense to ensure your savings, investments and other assets are in order in the event that you or your partner may need long-term care in the future.

If you are of working age, you are in the best position to plan for your future care needs. Accumulating wealth through investments or savings while you are earning will help with the potential costs of long-term care in later life.

What should you think about when planning for future care needs

- Who in your family may most need long- term care and for how long?
- Do you or another family member need to make long-term care provision now?
- Do you have sufficient money to pay for future long-term care fees?
- How long might you need to pay for a care fees plan?
- Is there the likelihood that home care or a nursing home may be required?
- What activities may you require help with, for example, help with dressing, using the toilet, feeding or mobility?
- Would your home require additional features such as a stair lift, an opening and closing bath, or a bath chair?

Chapter eleven
Protecting yourself from scams

Fraudsters are getting more deceitful and ever more successful. Pension and investment scams are on the increase in the UK. Everyday fraudsters are using sophisticated ways to part savers from their money, and the Internet and advances in digital communications mean these kinds of scams are getting more common and harder to identify. A lifetime's savings can be lost in moments.

Nearly one in ten over-55s fear they have been targeted by suspected scammers since the launch of pension freedoms, new research[1] shows.

Tactics commonly used to defraud
The study found 9% of over-55s say they have been approached about their pension funds by people they now believe to be scammers since the rules came into effect from April 2015. Offers to unlock or transfer funds are tactics commonly used to defraud people of their retirement savings.

One in three (33%) over-55s say the risk of being defrauded of their savings is a major concern following pension freedoms. However, nearly half (49%) of those approached say they did not report their concerns because they did not know how to or were unaware of who they could report the scammers to.

Reporting suspected scammers to authorities
Most recent pension fraud data[2] from ActionFraud, the national fraud and cybercrime reporting service, shows 991 cases have been reported since the launch of pension freedoms involving losses of more than £22.687 million

Alternative investments such as wine offered
The research found fewer than one in five (18%) of those approached by suspected scammers had reported their fears to authorities. Nearly half (47%) said the approaches involved offers to unlock pension funds or access money early, and 44% said they involved transferring pensions.

About 28% of those targeted by suspected fraudsters were offered alternative investments such as wine, and 20% say they were offered overseas investments, while 13% say scammers had suggested investing in crypto currencies. Around 6% believe they have been victims of fraud.

Safeguarding hard-earned retirement savings
Pension freedoms, though enormously popular with consumers, have created a potentially lucrative opportunity for fraudsters, and people need to be vigilant to safeguard their hard-earned retirement savings.

If it sounds too good to be true, then it usually is, and people should be sceptical of investments that are offering unusually high rates of return or which invest in unorthodox products which may be difficult to understand. If in any doubt, seeking professional financial advice from a regulated adviser will help ensure you don't get caught out.

Source data:
The Financial Services Compensation Scheme.

Some scammers have very convincing websites and other online presence, which make them look like a legitimate company. Always check with the FCA to make sure they're registered

Top five financial scams to look out for in the UK

1. Boiler-room schemes
These scams promise investors impressive returns, but they deliver nothing apart from a great big loss. More than 5,000 investors lost a combined £1.73 billion through boiler-room schemes reported to the Action Fraud crime-prevention centre in 2014. Victims will receive a telephone call out of the blue and be offered an investment opportunity with sky-high returns of as much as 40%. You will most likely be told that you must act fast and asked to transfer your money straight away. It's common for victims to part with tens of thousands of pounds. Boiler rooms are not authorised by the Financial Conduct Authority (FCA). This means that if you hand over your cash, it might be the last you will see of it.

Take Action
Check the FCA status of any firm you intend to deal with for investments. Call 0800 1116768 or go to www.fca.org.uk/register.

2. Phishing/smishing
The most common scams come from fraudsters posing as someone official, such as your bank or building society. Typically, you receive an email or text asking you to click a link and verify login, account and password details. The communication received is from a fraudster who will be able to read the information you type in, should you fall for their trick. This information is then used to raid your account. If you lose money this way, you won't get it back.

Take Action

Your bank will never ask you to disclose full security and password details, so alarm bells should ring. If in doubt, call your bank and ask them if they have tried to contact you.

3. Pension liberation

Scammers are bombarding people aged 55 and over with bogus investment opportunities to try to get hold of their pension savings.
One of the most common scams since the pension freedoms were announced involves alleged investment opportunities abroad
Low interest rates are tempting some people to take extra risks, so they are vulnerable to such fake investments. Fraudsters can approach you by post, email or telephone.

Take Action

If you're offered a 'must-have' investment or a free pension 'review' out of the blue, be wary. Also, be concerned if you're warned that the deal is limited and you must act now. Choosing the right retirement income product is a big decision and shouldn't be done quickly or under pressure.

Consult a registered professional financial adviser. If you think that you may have been made a fraudulent offer, contact Action Fraud on 0300 1232040 or visit the FCA's Scam Smart site to see if the investment you've been offered is on their warning list: http://scamsmart.fca.org.uk/warninglist.

4. Homebuying fraud

This con intercepts cash transferred as a home deposit to a solicitor in the lead-up to exchange and completion. It's all done via the Internet where a computer hacker monitors emails sent between a solicitor and client. When a bank transfer is about to be made, the fraudster emails the homebuyer pretending to be the solicitor, telling them the details of the law firm's bank account have changed. The unsuspecting homebuyer sends their cash to the new account, where it is withdrawn by the fraudsters.

Take Action

If you're buying a property, watch for any emails about payments, such as a change in bank details at the last minute. Many victims are told that the account is being 'audited', and so another one must be used. Ring your solicitor if you're in any doubt.

5. Freebie scams

Seemingly free trial offers for products are duping consumers out of millions of pounds a year. To get the freebies, you need to enter your card details – although told you won't be charged for the introductory period. In fact, you are often signing up to an expensive monthly subscription that is very difficult to get out of. Once this type of billing is approved – known as 'continuous payment authorisation' – up to £100 a month can be taken without any further contact.

Take Action

Report such free trial offers to The Advertising Standards Authority contact 020 7492 2222 or to make a complaint visit https://www.asa.org. uk/make-a-complaint.html

The Foundation provides local financial resources in the form of gifts to youth clubs, schools and organisations.

We fund structured, purposeful projects and ventures in and around Shropshire and Cheshire, giving youths the opportunity of reaching their full potential.

Work we have supported for the community

We have supported many projects that have positively impacted many groups of people within the community we have donated to date over £25,000 to:

Team funding, Sports equipment and kits, Charity fundraising activities, School projects, Guides, Scouts and Youth Clubs.

Please donate now and help us continue with our good work...

Every pound you put in is a pound that is given out.

All running costs are covered.

Glossary of Financial Terms

A

Alpha

Alpha is a measure of a fund's over or under performance compared to its benchmark. It represents the return of the fund when the benchmark is assumed to have a return of zero. It shows the extra value that the manager's activities seem to have contributed. If the Alpha is 5, the fund has outperformed its benchmark by 5% and the greater the Alpha, the greater the out performance.

Alternative Assets

Includes private real estate, public real estate, venture capital, non-venture private equity, hedge funds, distressed securities, oil and gas partnerships, event arbitrage, general arbitrage, managed funds, commodities, timber and other.

American Stock Exchange

AMEX is the second-largest stock exchange in the U.S., after the New York Stock Exchange (NYSE). In general, the listing rules are a little more lenient than those of the NYSE, and thus the AMEX has a larger representation of stocks and bonds issued by smaller companies than the NYSE. Some index options and interest rate options trading also occurs on the AMEX. The AMEX started as an alternative to the NYSE. It originated when brokers began meeting on the curb outside the NYSE in order to trade stocks that failed to meet the Big Board's stringent listing requirements, but the AMEX now has its own trading floor. In 1998, the parent company of the NASDAQ purchased the AMEX and combined their markets, although the two continue to operate separately. Also called The Curb.

Annual Rate of Return

There are several ways of calculating this. The most commonly used methodologies reflect the compounding effect of each period's increase or decrease from the previous period.

Annual Percentage Rate (APR)
The APR is designed to measure the "true cost of a loan". The aim is to create a level playing field for lenders preventing them from advertising a low rate and hiding fees. In the case of a mortgage the APR should reflect the yearly cost of a mortgage, including interest, mortgage insurance, and the origination fee, expressed as a percentage.

Annual Premium Equivalent
Calculated as regular premiums plus 10% of single premiums.

Arbitrage
A financial transaction or strategy that seeks to profit from a price differential perceived with respect to related or correlated instruments in different markets. Typically involves the simultaneous purchase of an instrument in one market and the sale of the same or related instrument in another market.

Asset Allocation
Apportioning of investment funds among categories of assets such as cash equivalents, stock, fixed-income investments, alternative investments such as hedge funds and managed futures funds, and tangible assets like real estate, precious metals and collectibles.

Average Monthly Gain
The average of all the profitable months of the fund.

Average Monthly Loss
The average of all the negative months of the fund.

Average Monthly Return
The average of all the monthly performance numbers of the fund.

B

Basis Point
A basis point is one one-hundredth of a percent i.e. 50 basis points or "bps" is 0.5%.

Bear / Bear Market
Bear is a term describing an investor who thinks that a market will decline. The term also refers to a short position held by a market maker. A Bear Market is a market where prices are falling over an extended period.

Bellwether
A stock or bond that is widely believed to be an indicator of the overall market's condition. Also known as Barometer stock.

Beta
Beta is a measure of a fund's volatility compared to its benchmark, or how sensitive it is to market movements. A fund with a Beta close to 1 means that the fund will move generally in line with the benchmark. Higher than 1 and the fund is more volatile than the benchmark, so that with a Beta of 1.5, say, the fund will be expected to rise or fall 1.5 points for every 1 point of benchmark movement. If this Beta is an advantage in a rising market – a 15% gain for every 10% rise in the benchmark –the reverse is true when markets fall. This is when managers will look for Betas below 1, so that in a down market the fund will not perform as badly as its benchmark.

Bid Price
The price at which an investor may sell units of a fund back to the fund manager. It is also the price at which a market maker will buy shares.

Blue Chips
Large, continuously well performing stock, presumed to be among the safer investments on an exchange.

Bond

A debt investment, with which the investor loans money to an entity (company or Government) that borrows the funds for a defined period of time at a specified interest rate. The indebted entity issues investors a certificate, or bond, that states the interest rate (coupon rate) that will be paid and when the loaned funds are to be returned (maturity date). Interest on bonds is usually paid every six-months.

Bond Rating Codes

Rating	S&P	Moody's
Highest quality	AAA	Aaa
High quality	AA	Aa
Upper medium quality	A	A
Medium grade	BBB	Baa
Somewhat speculative	BB	Ba
Low grade, speculative	B	B
Low grade, default possible	CCC	Caa
Low grade, partial recovery possible	CC	Ca
Default, recovery unlikely	C	C

Bottom up Investing

An approach to investing which seeks to identify well performing individual securities before considering the impact of economic trends.

BRIC

A term used to refer to the combination of Brazil, Russia, India and China. General consensus is that the term was first prominently used in a thesis of the Goldman Sachs Investment Bank. The main point of this 2003 paper was to argue that the economies of the BRICs are rapidly developing and by the year 2050 will eclipse most of the current richest countries of the world. Due to the popularity of the Goldman Sachs thesis, "BRIC" and "BRIMC" (M for Mexico), these terms are also extended to "BRICS" (S for South Africa) and "BRICKET" (including Eastern Europe and Turkey) and have become more generic terms to refer to these emerging markets.

Bull / Bull Market

An investor who believes that the market is likely to rise. A Bull Market is a market where prices are rising over an extended period.

Bulldog Bond

A sterling denominated bond that is issued in London by a company that is not British. These sterling bonds are referred to as bulldog bonds as the bulldog is a national symbol of England.

C

Child Trust Fund

A Child Trust Fund is a savings and investment account for children. Children born on or after 1st September 2002 will receive a £250 voucher to start their account. The account belongs to the child and can't be touched until they turn 18, so that children have some money behind them to start their adult life. Payments or contributions can be made up to a maximum of £1,200 per 12 month period (starting on the birthday of the child), excluding the voucher amount. Interest and capital growth will be earned tax-free. Additional deposits can be made by parents, grandparents or anyone else.

Closed-end Fund

Type of fund that has a fixed number of shares or units. Unlike open-ended mutual funds, closed-end funds do not stand ready to issue and redeem shares on a continuous basis.

Collar

A contract that protects the holder from a rise or fall in interest rates or some other underlying security above or below certain fixed points. The contract offers the investor protection from interest rate moves outside of an expected range.

Constant Proportion Portfolio Insurance CPPI

Strategy that basically buys shares as they rise and sells shares as they fall. To implement a CPPI strategy, the investor selects a floor below which the portfolio value is not allowed to fall. The floor increases in value at the rate of return on cash. If you think of the difference between the assets and floor as a "cushion", then the

CPPI decision rule is to simply keep the exposure to shares a constant multiple of the cushion.

Consumer Discretionary Sector

The array of businesses included in the Consumer Discretionary Sector are categorized into five industry groups. They are: Automobiles and Components; Consumer Durables and Apparel; Hotels, Restaurants and Leisure; Media; and Retailing.

Consumer Staples

The industries that manufacture and sell food/beverages, tobacco, prescription drugs and household products. Proctor and Gamble would be considered a consumer staple company because many of its products are household and food related.

Convertible Arbitrage

This is an investment strategy that involves taking a long position on a convertible security and a short position in its converting common stock. This strategy attempts to exploit profits when there is a pricing error made in the conversion factor of the convertible security.

Convertible Bond

A bond that can be exchanged, at the option of the holder, for a specific number of shares of the company's preferred stock or common stock. Convertibility affects the performance of the bond in certain ways. First and foremost, convertible bonds tend to have lower interest rates than nonconvertibles because they also accrue value as the price of the underlying stock rises. In this way, convertible bonds offer some of the benefits of both stocks and bonds. Convertibles earn interest even when the stock is trading down or sideways, but when the stock prices rise, the value of the convertible increases. Therefore, convertibles can offer protection against a decline in stock price. Because they are sold at a premium over the price of the stock, convertibles should be expected to earn that premium back in the first three or four years after purchase.

Core Fund
Fund that takes a middle of the road approach to generate returns for shareholders. These funds are generally structured in two ways. One strategy is to combine stocks and bonds (and possible income trusts) into a single fund to achieve a steady return and improved asset allocation. The other approach is to combine growth stocks and value stocks to diversify the risk from the typical ups and downs of markets. This type of fund can also be called a blend fund since it can show characteristics of a pure growth fund or a pure value fund. Either way, a core fund is focused to producing long-term results.

Corporate Bonds
Corporate Bonds are similar to gilts but are a form of borrowing by companies rather than Governments. Let's say Astra Zeneca wished to borrow a billion pounds for research and development. They would initially approach their brokers who would review the strength of Astra Zeneca versus the Government to assess what is a reasonable "risk premium". A secure company might be able to borrow money at 1 or 2 percentage points above the gilt rate and a very insecure company may have to pay 10 percentage points above the Government rate or in some cases substantially more. Companies' security is generally graded from AAA to no rating, the less secure debt being known in the UK as "High Yield", or as it is more accurately described by Americans as "Junk Bonds". So with Corporate Bonds the short term returns will vary in line with interest rates as they do with gilts, but also in line with the perceived strength of the company.

Correlation
A standardised measure of the relative movement between two variables, such as the price of a fund and an index. The degree of correlation between two variables is measured on a scale of −1 to +1. If two variables move up or down together, they are positively correlated. If they tend to move in opposite directions, they are negatively correlated.

Coupon
Denotes the rate of interest on a fixed interest security. A 10 % coupon pays interest of 10 % a year on the nominal value of the stock.

Cyclical Stock
The stock of a company which is sensitive to business cycles and whose performance is strongly tied to the overall economy. Cyclical companies tend to make products or provide services that are in lower demand during downturns in the economy and higher demand during upswings. Examples include the automobile, steel, and housing industries. The stock price of a cyclical company will often rise just before an economic upturn begins, and fall just before a downturn begins. Investors in cyclical stocks try to make the largest gains by buying the stock at the bottom of a business cycle, just before a turnaround begins. Opposite of defensive stock.

D

Debenture
A loan raised by a company, paying a fixed rate of interest and secured on the assets of the company.

Defensive Stock
A stock that tends to remain stable under difficult economic conditions. Defensive stocks include food, tobacco, oil, and utilities. These stocks hold up in hard times because demand does not decrease as dramatically as it may in other sectors. Defensive stocks tend to lag behind the rest of the market during economic expansion because demand does not increase as dramatically in an upswing.

Delta
The rate at which the price of an option changes in response to a move in the price of the underlying security. If an option's delta is 0.5 (out of a maximum of 1), a $2 move in the price of the underlying will produce a $1 move in the option.

Delta Hedge
A hedging position that causes a portfolio to be delta neutral.

Derivatives
Financial contracts whose value is tied to an underlying asset. Derivatives include futures and options.

Discount
When a security is selling below its normal market price, opposite of premium.

Distressed Securities
A distressed security is a security of a company which is currently in default, bankruptcy, financial distress or a turnaround situation.

E

Efficient Frontier
A line created from the risk-reward graph, comprised of optimal portfolios. The optimal portfolios plotted along the curve have the highest expected return possible for the given amount of risk.

EFTA – European Fair Trade Association
A network of 11 Fair Trade organisations in nine European countries which import Fair Trade products from some 400 economically disadvantaged producer groups in Africa, Asia and Latin America. EFTA's members are based in Austria, Belgium, France, Germany, Italy, the Netherlands, Spain, Switzerland and the United Kingdom.

Embedded Value EV
A method of accounting used by life insurance business. The embedded value is the sum of the net assets of the insurance business under conventional accounting and the present value of the in-force business based on estimates of future cash flows and conservative assumptions about for example, mortality, persistence and expenses. Accounts users prefer this method because it gives a separate indication of new business profitability, a key performance indicator for a life insurer.

Emerging Markets
Typically includes markets within countries that have an underdeveloped or developing infrastructure with significant potential for economic growth and increased capital market participation for foreign investors. These countries generally possess some of the following characteristics; per capita GNP less than $9000, recent economic liberalisation, debt ratings below investment grade, recent liberalisation of the political system and non membership of the Organisation of Economic Cooperation and Development. Because many emerging countries do not allow short selling or offer viable futures or other derivatives products with which to hedge, emerging market investing entails investing in geographic regions that have underdeveloped capital markets and exhibit high growth rates and high rates of inflation. Investing in emerging markets can be very volatile and may also involve currency risk, political risk and liquidity risk. Generally a long-only investment strategy.

Emerging Markets Debt
Debt instruments of emerging market countries. Most bonds are US Dollar denominated and a majority of secondary market trading is in Brady bonds.

Equities
Ownership positions in companies that can be traded in public markets. Often produce current income which is paid in the form of quarterly dividends. In the event of the company going bankrupt equity holders' claims are subordinate to the claims of preferred stockholders and bondholders.

Equity Hedge
Also known as long / short equity, combines core long holdings of equities with short sales of stock or stock index options. Equity hedge portfolios may be anywhere from net long to net short depending on market conditions. Equity hedge managers generally increase net long exposure in bull markets and decrease net long exposure or are even net short in a bear market.

Equity Market Neutral

This investment strategy is designed to exploit equity market inefficiencies and usually involves being simultaneously long and short equity portfolios of the same size within a country. Market neutral portfolios are designed to be either beta or currency neutral or both. Attempts are often made to control industry, sector and market capitalisation exposures.

Equity Risk

The risk of owning stock or having some other form of ownership interest.

Ethical Investing

Choosing to invest in companies that operate ethically, provide social benefits, and are sensitive to the environment. Also called socially conscious investing.

EU

European Union. The economic association of over a dozen European countries which seek to create a unified, barrier-free market for products and services throughout the continent. The majority of countries share a common currency with a unified authority over that currency. Notable exceptions to the common currency are the UK, Sweden, Norway, Denmark.

Eurobond

A bond issued and traded outside the country whose currency it is denominated in, and outside the regulations of a single country; usually a bond issued by a non-European company for sale in Europe. Interest is paid gross.

Eurozone or Euroland

The collective group of countries which use the Euro as their common currency.

Event Driven Investing

Investment strategy seeking to identify and exploit pricing inefficiencies that have been caused by some sort of corporate event such as a merger, spin-off, distressed situation or recapitalisation.

Exit Fee

A fee paid to redeem an investment. It is a charge levied for cashing in a fund's capital.

Exposure

The condition of being subjected to a source of risk.

F

FCP

Fonds Commun de Placement. FCPs are a common fund structure in Luxembourg. In contrast to SICAV, they are not companies, but are organised as co-ownerships and must be managed by a fund management company.

Feeder Fund

A fund which invests only in another fund. The feeder fund may be a different currency to the main fund and may be used to channel cash in to the main fund for a different currency class.

Fixed Interest

The term fixed interest is often used by banks and building societies relating to an account that pays a set rate of interest for a set time period. This type of investment is capital secure and the returns are known at outset. However, fixed interest within the investment world is a completely different concept. It is used to describe funds that invest in Government Gilts and Corporate Bond securities.

Fixed Income Arbitrage

Investment strategy that seeks to exploit pricing inefficiencies in fixed income securities and their derivative instruments. Typical investment is long a fixed income security or related instrument that is perceived to be undervalued and short a similar related fixed income security or related instrument. Often highly leveraged.

Floating Rate

Any interest rate that changes on a periodic basis. The change is usually tied to movement of an outside indicator, such as the Bank of England Base Rate. Movement above or below certain levels is often prevented by a predetermined floor and ceiling for a given rate. For example, you might see a rate set at "base plus 2%". This means that the rate on the loan will always be 2% higher than the base rate, which changes regularly to take into account changes in the inflation rate. For an individual taking out a loan when rates are low, a fixed rate loan would allow him or her to "lock in" the low rates and not be concerned with fluctuations. On the other hand, if interest rates were historically high at the time of the loan, he or she would benefit from a floating rate loan, because as the prime rate fell to historically normal levels, the rate on the loan would decrease. Also called adjustable rate.

Floor
   A contract that protects the holder against a decline in interest rates or prices below a certain point.

Forward
   An agreement to execute a transaction at some time in the future. In the foreign exchange market this is a tailor made deal where an investor agrees to buy or sell an amount of currency at a given date.

Forward Rate Agreement (FRA)
   A type of forward contract that is linked to interest rates.

FTSE 100
   The Financial Times Stock Exchange 100 stock index, a market cap weighted index of stocks traded on the London Stock Exchange. Similar to the S&P 500 in the United States.

Fund of Funds
   An investment vehicle that invests in more than one fund. Portfolio will typically diversify across a variety of investment managers, investment strategies and subcategories. Provides investors with access to managers with higher minimums than individuals might otherwise afford.

Funds under Management
   Total amount of funds managed by an entity, excluding

G

Gearing
   The effect that borrowing has on the equity capital of a company or the asset value of a fund. If the assets bought with funds borrowed appreciate in value, the excess of value over funds borrowed will accrue to the shareholder, thus augmenting, or gearing up the value of their investment.

Geographic Spread
   The distribution in a fund's portfolio over different parts of the world, either by countries or larger areas.

Gilt-Edged Securities
   Stocks and shares issued and guaranteed by the British government to raise funds and traded on the Stock Exchange. A relatively risk-free investment, gilts bear fixed interest and are usually redeemable on a specified date. The term is now used generally to describe securities of the highest value. According to the redemption date, gilts are described as short (up to five years), medium, or long (15 years or more).

Gilts
   Gilts are effectively Government borrowing. When the Chancellor does not have sufficient income to meet his expenditure, then the Government will often borrow money in the form of gilts. These can be for a variety of different terms, paying a range of interest rates.

A typical example would be a ten year gilt which may pay, say, 5% income. This is the most secure investment you could buy, as you know the rate of return and you know when you will receive your capital back. The UK Government has never defaulted on a gilt.

If however you wanted to access your money before maturity then you would have to sell your gilt on the open market. Let's say you were trying to sell your gilt after one year. In order to obtain a value any potential purchaser will look at the term remaining on your gilt and the interest rate promised, and compare this to new gilts being launched at the time. If the Government was then launching a new gilt over a nine year time period, and promising to pay 6% per annum, then clearly nobody is going to want to pay the same amount of money for your gilt which is offering a lower interest rate.

They would probably therefore offer at least 9% less than you originally paid for it to reflect the 1% difference in income over the nine years of the remaining term. So whilst you had set out to achieve guaranteed returns, if you sell a gilt before maturity you could potentially make a capital loss on it, in this instance a loss of 9% over the year.

However, if you decide to keep the gilt until its maturity you will still receive all of your interest and the capital back. Having said this, your valuation each year will vary depending on market conditions.

GNMA (Ginnie Mae)
Government National Mortgage Association. A U.S. Government-owned agency which buys mortgages from lending institutions, securitizes them, and then sells them to investors. Because the payments to investors are guaranteed by the full faith and credit of the U.S. Government, they return slightly less interest than other mortgage-backed securities.

Growth Stocks
Stock of a company which is growing earnings and/or revenue faster than its industry or the overall market. Such companies usually pay little or no dividends, preferring to use the income instead to finance further expansion.

Growth Orientated Portfolios
Dominant theme is growth in revenues, earnings and market share. Many of these portfolios are hedged to mitigate against declines in the overall market.

Global Macro
The investment strategy is based on shifts in global economies. Derivatives are often used to speculate on currency and interest rate movements.

Guided Architecture
In relation to funds, for example FPIL Premier policyholders may only go into the FPIL mirror fund range – this is guided architecture. In contrast to FPIL Reserve policyholders who may choose any security – open architecture.

H

Hawk
An investor who has a negative view towards inflation and its effects on markets. Hawkish investors prefer higher interest rates in order to maintain reduced inflation.

Hedge
Any transaction with the objective of limiting exposure to risk such as changes in exchange rates or prices.

Hedge Fund
A pooled investment vehicle that is privately organised, administered by investment management professionals and generally not widely available to the general public. Many hedge funds share a number of characteristics; they hold long and short positions, use leverage to enhance returns, pay performance or incentive fees to their managers, have high minimum investment requirements and target absolute returns. Generally, hedge funds are not constrained by legal limitations on their investment discretion and can adopt a variety of trading strategies. The hedge fund manager often has its own capital (or that of its principals) invested in the hedge fund it manages.

Herding
Hedge fund managers while taking a position may encourage other investors to follow this trend.

High Conviction Stock Picking
A typical portfolio is not constrained by benchmarks, allowing the manager to pursue an approach where a smaller number of stocks are chosen that may bear little or no resemblance to the consensus view. i.e the manager's conviction.

High Water Mark
The assurance that a fund only takes fees on profits actually earned by an individual investment. For example, a £10 million investment is made in year one and the fund declines by 50%, leaving £5 million in the fund. In year two, the fund returns 100% bringing the investment value back to £10 million. If a fund has a high water mark it will not take incentive fees on the return in year two since the investment has never grown. The fund will only take incentive fees if the investment grows above the initial level of £10 million.

High-Yield Bond
Often called junk bonds, these are low grade fixed income securities of companies that show significant upside potential. The bond has to pay a high yield due to significant credit risk.

Hurdle Rate
The minimum investment return a fund must exceed before a performance-based incentive fee can be taken. For example if a fund has a hurdle rate of 10% and the fund returned 18% for the year, the fund will only take incentive fees on the 8 percentage points above the hurdle rate.

I

Index
An arithmetic mean of selected stocks intended to represent the behaviour of the market or some component of it. One example is the FTSE 100 which adds the current prices of the one hundred FTSE 100 stocks and divides the results by a pre-determined number, the divisor.

Index Funds
A fund that attempts to achieve a performance similar to that stated in an index. The purpose of this fund is to realise an investment return at least equal to the broad market covered by the indices while reducing management costs.

Index Linked Gilt
A gilt, the interest and capital of which change in line with the Retail Price Index.

In the Money
A condition where an option has a positive intrinsic value.

Intrinsic Value
A component of the market value of an option. If the strike price of a call option is cheaper than the prevailing market price, then the option has a positive intrinsic value, and is "in the money".

Investment Grade
Something classified as investment grade is, by implication, medium to high quality.
1) In the case of a stock, a firm that has a strong balance sheet, considerable   capitalization, and   is recognized as a leader in its industry.
2) In the case of fixed income, a bond with a rating of BBB or higher.

J

January Effect
Tendency of US stock markets to rise between December 31 and the end of the first week in January. The January Effect occurs because many investors choose to sell some of their stock right before the end of the year in order to claim a capital loss for tax purposes. Once the tax calendar rolls over to a new year on January 1st these same investors quickly reinvest their money in the market, causing stock prices to rise. Although the January Effect has been observed numerous times throughout history, it is difficult for

investors to profit from it since the market as a whole expects it to happen and therefore adjusts its prices accordingly.

Junk Bond
A bond that pays a high yield due to significant credit risk

L

Leverage
When investors borrow funds to increase the amount they have invested in a particular position, they use leverage. Sometimes managers use leverage to enable them to put on new positions without having to take off other positions prematurely. Managers who target very small price discrepancies or spreads will often use leverage to magnify the returns from these discrepancies. Leverage both magnifies the risk of the strategy as well as creates risk by giving the lender power over the disposition of the investment portfolio. This may occur in the form of increased margin requirements or adverse market shifts, forcing a partial or complete liquidation of the portfolio.

The amount of leverage used by the fund is commonly expressed as a percentage of the fund. For example if the fund has £1 million and borrows another £2 million to bring the total invested to £3 million, then the fund is leveraged 200%

Life Cycle Funds
Life-cycle funds are the closest thing the industry has to a maintenance-free retirement fund. Life-cycle funds, also referred to as "age-based funds" or "target-date funds", are a special breed of the balanced fund. They are a type of fund of funds structured between equity and fixed income. But the distinguishing feature of the life-cycle fund is that its overall asset allocation automatically adjusts to become more conservative as your expected retirement date approaches. While life-cycle funds have been around for a while, they have been gaining popularity.

LIBOR
London Inter Bank Offered Rate.

Liquidity
   1) The degree to which an asset or security can be bought or sold in the market without affecting the asset's price. Liquidity is characterized by a high level of trading activity.
   2) The ability to convert an asset to cash quickly.
   Investing in illiquid assets is riskier because there might not be a way for you to get your money out of the investment. Examples of assets with good liquidity include blue chip common stock and those assets in the money market. A fund with good liquidity would be characterised by having enough units outstanding to allow large transactions without a substantial change in price.

Liquidity Risk
   Risk from a lack of liquidity, ie an investor having difficulty getting their money out of an investment.

Listed Security
   Stock or bond that has been accepted for trading by an organised and registered securities exchange. Advantages of being listed are an orderly market place, more liquidity, fair price determination, accurate and continuous reporting on sales and quotations, information on listed companies and strict regulations for the protection of securities holders.

Lock Up / Lock In
   Time period during which an initial investment cannot be redeemed.

Long Position
   Holding a positive amount of an asset (or an asset underlying a derivative instrument)

Long / Short Hedged
   Also described as the Jones Model. Manager buys securities he believes will go up in price and sells short securities he believes will decline in price. Manager will be either net long or net short and may change the net position frequently. For example a manager may be 60% long and 100% short, giving him a market exposure of 40% net short. The basic belief behind this strategy is that it will enhance the

manager's stock picking ability and protect investors in all market conditions.

M

Macro-Economics
The field of economics that studies the behaviour of the economy as a whole. Macroeconomics looks at economy-wide phenomena such as changes in unemployment, national income, rate of growth, and price levels.

Managed Accounts
Accounts of individual investors which are managed individually by an investment manager. The minimum size is usually in excess of £3 million.

Managed Futures
An approach to fund management that uses positions in government securities, futures contracts, options on futures contracts and foreign exchange in a portfolio. Some managers specialise in physical commodity futures but most find they must trade a variety of financial and non-financial contracts if they have considerable assets under management.

Management Fee
The fees taken by the manager on the entire asset level of the investment. For example, if at the end of the period the investment is valued at £1 million and the management fee is 1.2%, then the fee would be £12,000.

Margin
The amount of assets that must be deposited in a margin account in order to secure a portion of a party's obligations under a contract. For example, to buy or sell an exchange traded futures contract, a party must post a specified amount that is determined by the exchange, referred to as initial margin. In addition, a party will be required to post variation margin if the futures contracts change in value. Margin is also required in connection with the purchase and

sale of securities where the full purchase price is not paid up front or the securities sold are not owned by the seller.

Market Maker
An Exchange member firm that is obliged to make a continuous two way price, that is to offer to buy and sell securities in which it is registered throughout the mandatory quote period.

Market Neutral Investing
An investment strategy that aims to produce almost the same profit regardless of market circumstances, often by taking a combination of long and short positions. This approach relies on the manager's ability to make money through relative valuation analysis, rather than through market direction forecasting. The strategy attempts to eliminate market risk and be profitable in any market condition.

Market Risk
Risk from changes in market prices

Market Timing
1) An accepted practice of allocating assets among investments by switching into investments that appear to be beginning an up trend, and switching out of investments that appear to be starting a downtrend.
2) An increasingly unacceptable / illegal practice of undertaking frequent or large transactions in mutual funds. Especially where there is a time difference between the close of the relevant markets that the fund invests in and the valuation of the fund. ie a Far East fund that is valued the next day in the UK.

Market Value
The value at which an asset trades, or would trade in the market.

Mark to Market
When the value of securities in a portfolio are updated to reflect the changes that have occurred due to the movement of the

underlying market. The security will then be valued at its current market price.

Maximum Draw Down
The largest loss suffered by a security or fund, peak to trough, over a given period, usually one month.

Merger Arbitrage
Sometimes called Risk Arbitrage, involves investment in event-driven situations such as leveraged buy outs, mergers and hostile takeovers. Normally the stock of an acquisition target appreciates while the acquiring company's stock decreases in value.

Mezzanine Level
Stage of a company's development just prior to its going public. Venture capitalists entering at that point have a lower risk of loss than at previous stages and can look forward to early capital appreciation as a result of the market value gained by an initial public offering.

Micro-Economics
The behaviour and purchasing decisions of individuals and firms.

Money Market Funds
Mutual funds that invest in short term highly liquid money market instruments. These funds are used when preservation of capital is paramount. They may be used to "park" money between investments, especially during periods of market uncertainty.

Mortgage Backed Security
A pass-through security that aggregates a pool of mortgage-backed debt obligations. Mortgage-backed securities' principal amounts are usually government guaranteed. Homeowners' principal and interest payments pass from the originating bank through a government agency or investment bank, to investors, net of a loan servicing fee payable to the originator.

Multi-Manager Product

An investment pool that allocates assets to a number of managers with different investment styles. This methodology facilitates a high degree of diversification and accordingly the potential for a greater spread of risk. Hedge funds often have this structure. Smaller investors are able to enjoy access to a greater variety of managers that would normally be prohibited by minimum investment requirements for each manager. Funds of funds are a classic multi-manager product.

Municipal Bond (USA)

A debt security issued by a state, municipality, or county, in order to finance its capital expenditures. Municipal bonds are exempt from federal taxes and from most state and local taxes, especially if you live in the state the bond is issued. Such expenditures might include the construction of highways, bridges or schools. "Munis" are bought for their favourable tax implications, and are popular with people
in high income tax brackets.

Mutual Fund

A security that gives small investors access to a well diversified portfolio of equities, bonds, and other securities. Each shareholder participates in the gain or loss of the fund. Shares are issued and can be redeemed as needed. The fund's net asset value (NAV) is determined each day. Each mutual fund portfolio is invested to match the objective stated in the prospectus. Some examples of mutual funds are UK Unit Trusts, Open-ended Investment Companies (OEICs), EU registered UCITS, Luxembourg based SICAVs.

N

NAREIT

National Association of Real Estate Investment Trusts

Nasdaq

A computerised system established by the NASD to facilitate trading by providing broker/dealers with current bid and ask price quotes on over-the-counter stocks and some listed stocks. Unlike the Amex and the NYSE, the Nasdaq (once an acronym for the National Association of securities Dealers Automated Quotation system) does not have a physical trading floor that brings together buyers and sellers. Instead, all trading on the Nasdaq exchange is done over a network of computers and telephones. Also, the Nasdaq does not employ market specialists to buy unfilled orders like the NYSE does. The Nasdaq began when brokers started informally trading via telephone; the network was later formalized and linked by computer in the early 1970s. In 1998 the parent company of the Nasdaq purchased the Amex, although the two continue to operate separately. Orders for stock are sent out electronically on the Nasdaq, where market makers list their buy and sell prices. Once a price is agreed upon, the transaction is executed electronically.

Net Asset Value (NAV)
NAV equals the closing market value of all assets within a portfolio after subtracting all liabilities including accrued fees and expenses. NAV per share is the NAV divided by the number of shares in issue. This is often used as the price of a fund. A purchase fee may be added to the NAV when buying units in the fund. This fee is typically 1-7%.

Net Exposure
The exposure level of a fund to the market. It is calculated by subtracting the short percentage from the long percentage. For example if a fund is 100% long and 30% short, then the net exposure is 70% long.

Nominee Name
Name in which a security is registered and held in trust on behalf of the beneficial owner.

O

Offer Price
The price at which a fund manager or market maker will sell shares to you. (ie offer them to you). The offer price is higher than the Bid Price which is the price at which they will buy shares from

you. (ie they will make a bid). This is one way in which a market maker turns a profit. A fund manager may use the difference to cover dealing administration costs.

Offshore
Located or based outside of one's national boundaries. Typically these locations have preferential tax treatments and fund legislation.

Open Architecture
In relation to funds, for example FPIL Reserve policyholders may choose any security – open architecture. In contrast to FPIL Premier policyholders who may only go into the FPIL mirror fund range – this is guided architecture.

Open-ended Funds
These are funds where units or shares can be bought and sold daily and where the number of units or shares in issue can vary daily.

Opportunistic Investing
A general term describing any fund that is opportunistic in nature. These types of funds are usually aggressive and seek to make money in the most efficient way at any given time. Investment themes are dominated by events that are seen as special situations or short-term opportunities to capitalise from price fluctuations or imbalances, such as initial public offering.

Option
A privilege sold by one party to another that offers the buyer the right, but not the obligation, to buy (call)or sell (put) a security at an agreed-upon price during a certain period of time or on a specific date. Options are extremely versatile securities that can be used in many different ways. Traders use optionsto speculate, which is a relatively risky practice, while hedgers use options to reduce the risk of holding an asset.

Over the Counter- OTC
A security traded in some context other than on a formal exchange such as the LSE, NYSE, DJIA, TSX, AMEX, etc. A stock is traded over the counter usually because the company is small and

unable to meet listing requirements of the exchanges. Also known as unlisted stock, these securities are traded by brokers/dealers who negotiate directly with one another over computer networks and by phone. The Nasdaq, however, is also considered to be an OTC market, with the tier 1 being represented bycompanies such as Microsoft, Dell and Intel. Instruments such as bonds do not trade on a formal exchange and are thus considered over-the- counter securities. Most debt instruments are traded byinvestment banks making markets for specific issues. If someone wants to buy or sell a bond, they callthe bank that makes the market in that bond and ask for quotes. Many derivative instruments such as forwards, swaps and most exotic derivatives are also traded OTC.

Out of the Money

This refers to options :
1) For a call, when an option's strike price is higher than the market price of the underlying stock.
2) For a put, when the strike price is below the market price of the underlying stock.
Basically, an option that would be worthless if it expired today.

Over-Hedging

Locking in a price, such as through a futures contract, for more goods, commodities or securities that is required to protect a position. While hedging does protect a position, over-hedging can be costly in the form of missed opportunities. Although you can lock in a selling price, over-hedging might result in a producer or seller missing out on favourable market prices. For example, if you entered into a January futures contract to sell 25,000 shares of 'Smith Holdings' at $6.50 per share you would not be able to take advantage if the spot price jumped to $7.00.

Overlay Strategy

A type of derivatives strategy. This strategy is often employed to provide protection from currencies or interest rate movements that are not the primary focus of the main portfolio strategy.

Overweight
Refers to an investment position that is larger than the generally accepted benchmark. For example, if a company normally holds a portfolio whose weighting of cash is 10%, and then increases cash holdings to 15%, the portfolio would have an overweight position in cash.

P

Pair Trading
The strategy of matching a long position with a short position in two stocks of the same sector. This creates a hedge against the sector and the overall market that the two stocks are in. The hedge createdis essentially a bet that you are placing on the two stocks; the stock you are long in versus the stock you are short in. It's the ultimate strategy for stock pickers, because stock picking is all that counts. What the actual market does won't matter (much). If the market or the sector moves in one direction or the other, the gain on the long stock is offset by a loss on the short.

Percent Long
The percentage of a fund invested in long positions.

Percent Short
The percentage of a fund that is sold short.

Performance Fee
The fee payable to the fund adviser on new profits earned by the fund for the period.

Portfolio Turnover
The number of times an average portfolio security is replaced during an accounting period, usually a year.

Premium
The total cost of an option. The premium of an option is basically the sum of the option's intrinsic and time value. It is important to note that volatility also affects the premium.

The difference between the higher price paid for a fixed-income security and the security's face amount at issue. If a fixed-income security (bond) is purchased at a premium, existing interest rates are lower than the coupon rate. Investors pay a premium for an investment that will return an amount greater than existing interest rates.

Price Earnings Ratio (P/E Ratio)

A valuation ratio of a company's current share price compared to its per-share earnings. Calculated as: Market Value per Share/Earnings per Share (EPS)

EPS is usually from the last four quarters (trailing P/E), but sometimes can be taken from the estimates of earnings expected in the next four quarters (projected or forward P/E). A third variation is the sum of the last two actual quarters and the estimates of the next two quarters.

Sometimes the P/E is referred to as the "multiple," because it shows how much investors are willing to pay per dollar of earnings. In general, a high P/E means high projected earnings in the future. However, the P/E ratio actually doesn't tell us a whole lot by itself. It's usually only useful to compare the P/E ratios of companies in the same industry, or to the market in general, or against the company's own historical P/E.

Prime Broker

A broker which acts as settlement agent, provides custody for assets, provides financing for leverage, and prepares daily account statements for its clients, who might be money managers, hedge funds, market makers, arbitrageurs, specialists and other professional investors.

Private Placement / Private Equity

When equity capital is made available to companies or investors, but not quoted on a stock market. The funds raised through private equity can be used to develop new products and technologies, to expand working capital, to make acquisitions, or to strengthen a company's balance sheet. The average individual investor will not have access to private equity because it requires a very large investment. The result is the sale of securities to a relatively small number of investors. Private placements do not have to be registered with organizations such as the FSA, SEC because no public offering is involved.

Proprietary Trading

When a firm trades for direct gain instead of commission dollars. Essentially, the firm has decided to profit from the market rather than commissions from processing trades. Firms who engage in proprietary trading believe they have a competitive advantage that will enable them to earn excess returns.

Prospectus

In the case of mutual funds, a prospectus describes the fund's objectives, history, manager background, and financial statements. A prospectus makes investors aware of the risks of an investment and in most jurisdictions is required to be published by law.

Protected Cell Company

A standard limited company that has been separated into legally distinct portions or cells. The revenue streams, assets and liabilities of each cell are kept separate from all other cells. Each cell has its own separate portion of the PCC's overall share capital, allowing shareholders to maintain sole ownership of an entire cell while owning only a small proportion of the PCC as a whole. PCCs can provide a means of entry into a captive insurance market to entities for which it was previously uneconomic. The overheads of a protected cell captive can be shared between the owners of each of the cells, making the captive cheaper to run from the point of view of the insured.

Purification

The process whereby Muslims give to charity any interest deemed to have been credited to their holdings in funds or stocks.

Put Option

An option giving the holder the right, but not the obligation, to sell a specific quantity of an asset for a fixed price during a specific period.

Q

Qualitative Analysis

Analysis that uses subjective judgment in evaluating securities based on non-financial information such as management expertise, cyclicality of industry, strength of research and development, and labour relations.

Quantitative Analysis

A security analysis that uses financial information derived from company annual reports and income statements to evaluate an investment decision. Some examples are financial ratios, the cost of capital, asset valuation, and sales and earnings trends.

Quasi Sovereign Bond

Debt issued by a public sector entity that is, like a sovereign bond, guaranteed by the sovereign, however there is a difference in that there may be a timing difference in repayment in the unlikely event of default.

R

REIT Real Estate Investment Trust

A security that trades like a stock on the major exchanges and invests in real estate directly, through either properties or mortgages.

REITs receive special tax considerations and typically offer investors high yields, as well as a highly liquid method of investing in real estate. Equity REITs invest in and own properties (thus responsible for the equity or value of their real estate assets). Their revenues come principally from their properties' rents. Mortgage REITs deal in investment and ownership of property mortgages. These REITs loan money for mortgages to owners of real estate, or purchase existing mortgages or mortgage-backed securities. Their revenues are generated primarily by the interest that they earn on the mortgage loans. Hybrid REITs combine the investment strategies of equity REITs and mortgage REITs by investing in both properties and mortgages.

R – Squared

A statistical measure that represents the percentage of a fund's or security's movements that are explained by movements in a benchmark index. It is a measure of correlation with the benchmark.R-squared values range from 0 to 100. An R-squared of 100 means that all movements of a security are completely explained by movements in the index. ie perfect correlation.

Repurchase Agreement (Repo)

A form of short-term borrowing for dealers in government securities. The dealer sells the government securities to investors, usually on an overnight basis, and buys them back the following day. For the party selling the security (and agreeing to repurchase it in the future) it is a repo; for the party on the other end of the transaction (buying the security and agreeing to sell in the future) it is a reverse repurchase agreement. Repos are classified as a money-market instrument. They are usually used toraise short-term capital.

Risk Adjusted Rate of Return

A measure of how much risk a fund or portfolio took on to earn its returns, usually expressed as a number or a rating. This is often represented by the Sharpe Ratio. The more return per unit of risk, the better

Risk Arbitrage

A broad definition for three types of arbitrage that contain an element of risk:
1) Merger and Acquisition Arbitrage - The simultaneous purchase of stock in a company being acquired and the sale (or short sale) of stock in the acquiring company.
2) Liquidation Arbitrage - The exploitation of a difference between a company's current value and its estimated liquidation value.

3) Pairs Trading - The exploitation of a difference between two very similar companies in the same industry that have historically been highly correlated. When the two company's values diverge to a historically high level you can take an offsetting position in each (e.g. go long in one and short the other) because, as history has shown, they will inevitably come to be similarly valued.

In theory true arbitrage is riskless, however, the world in which we operate offers very few of these opportunities. Despite these forms of arbitrage being somewhat risky, they are still relatively low-risk trading strategies which money managers (mainly hedge fund managers) and retail investors alike can employ.

Risk-Free Rate

The quoted rate on an asset that has virtually no risk. The rate quoted for US treasury bills are widely used as the risk free rate.

Risk Reward Ratio

This is closely related to the Sharpe Ratio, except the risk reward ratio does not use a risk free rate in its calculation. The higher the risk reward ratio, the better. Calculated as : Annualised rate of return/Annualised Standard Deviation

S

Santa Claus Rally

The rise in US stock prices that sometimes occurs in the week after Christmas, often in anticipation of the January effect.

Satellite Fund

Specialist mandate fund that offers greater breadth of proposition than a "core" fund.

Secondary Market

A market in which an investor purchases an asset from another investor, rather than an issuing corporation. A good example is the London Stock Exchange. All stock exchanges are part of the secondary market, as investors buy securities from other investors instead of an issuing company.

Sector Fund

A mutual fund whose objective is to invest in a particular industry or sector of the economy to capitalizeon returns. Because most of the stocks in this type of fund are all in the same industry, there is a lack ofdiversification. The fund tends to do very well or not well at all, depending on the conditions of the specific sector.

Securities

General name for all stocks and shares of all types.

Securities Lending

When a brokerage lends securities owned by its clients to short sellers. This allows brokers to create additional revenue (commissions) on the short sale transaction.

Semi-gilt

A financial instrument through which a municipality or parastatal (owned or controlled wholly or partly by the government) borrows money from the public in exchange for a fixed repayment plan.

SICAV

SICAV stands for Societe D'Investissement a Capital Variable. It is a Luxembourg incorporated company that is responsible for the management of a mutual fund and manages a portfolio of securities. The share capital is equal to the net assets of the fund. The units in the portfolio are delivered as shares and the investors are referred to as shareholders. SICAVs are common fund structures in Luxembourg.

Sharia(h)

Sharia refers to the body of Islamic law. The term means "way" or "path"; it is the legal framework within which public and some private aspects of life are regulated for those living in a legal system based on Muslim principles.

Sharpe Ratio

A ratio developed by Bill Sharpe to measure risk-adjusted performance. It is calculated by subtracting the risk free rate from the rate of return for a portfolio and dividing the result by the standard deviation of the portfolio returns.

Calculated as: Expected Portfolio Return – Risk Free Rate/Portfolio Standard Deviation

The Sharpe ratio tells us whether the returns of a portfolio are because of smart investment decisions or a result of excess risk. The Sortino Ratio is a variation of this.

Short Selling

The selling of a security that the seller does not own, or any sale that is completed by the delivery of a security borrowed by the seller. Short sellers assume that they will be able to buy the stock at a lower amount than the price at which they sold short. Selling short is the opposite of going long. That is, short sellers make money if the stock goes down in price. This is an advanced trading strategy with many unique risks and pitfalls.

Small Caps

Stocks or funds with smaller capitalisation. They tend to be less liquid than blue chips, but they tend to have higher returns.

Soft Commissions

A means of paying brokerage firms for their services through commission revenue, as opposed to normal payments. For example, a mutual fund may offer to pay for the research of a brokerage firm by executing trades at the brokerage.

Sovereign Debt

A debt instrument guaranteed by a government.

Special Situations Investing

Strategy that seeks to profit from pricing discrepancies resulting from corporate event transactions such as mergers and acquisitions, spin-offs, bankruptcies or recapitalisations. Type of event-driven strategy.

Specific Risk

Risk that affects a very small number of assets. This is sometimes referred to as "unsystematic risk." An example would be news that is specific to either one stock or a small number of stocks, such as a sudden strike by the employees of a company you have shares in or a new governmental regulation affecting a particular group of companies. Unlike systematic risk or market risk, specific risk can be diversified away.

Spin Off
A new, independent company created through selling or distributing new shares for an existing part of another company. Spinoffs may be done through a rights offering.

Sponsors
Lead investors in a fund who supply the seed money. Often the general partner in a hedge fund.

Spread
1) The difference between the bid and the offer prices of a security or asset.
2) An options position established by purchasing one option and selling another option of the same class, but of a different series

Standard Deviation
Tells us how much the return on the fund is deviating from the expected normal returns.

Stop-Loss Order
An order placed with a broker to sell a security when it reaches a certain price. It is designed to limit an investor's loss on a security position. This is sometimes called a "stop market order." In other words, setting a stop-loss order for 10% below the price you paid for the stock would limit your loss to 10%.

Strategic Bond Funds
Invest primarily in higher yielding assets including high yield bonds, investment grade bonds, preference shares and other bonds. The funds take strategic asset allocation decisions between countries, asset classes, sectors and credit ratings.

Strike Price
The stated price per share for which underlying stock may be purchased (for a call) or sold (for a put) by the option holder upon exercise of the option contract.

Swap
Traditionally, the exchange of one security for another to change the maturity (bonds), quality of issues (stocks or bonds), or because investment objectives have changed. Recently, swaps have grown to include currency swaps and interest rates swaps. If firms in separate countries have comparative advantages on interest rates, then a swap could benefit both firms. For example, one firm may have a lower fixed interest rate, while another has access to a lower floating interest rate. These firms could swap to take advantage of the lower rates.

Swaption (Swap Option)
The option to enter into an interest rate swap. In exchange for an option premium, the buyer gains the right but not the obligation to enter into a specified swap agreement with the issuer on a specified future date.

Swing Trading (Swings)
A style of trading that attempts to capture gains in a stock within one to four days. To find situations in which a stock has this extraordinary potential to move in such a short time frame, the trader must act quickly. This is mainly used by at-home and day traders. Large institutions trade in sizes too big to move in and out of stocks quickly. The individual trader is able to exploit the short-term stock movements without the competition of major traders. Swing traders use technical analysis to look for stocks with short-term price momentum. These traders aren't interested in the fundamental or intrinsic value of stocks but rather in their price trends and patterns.

Systematic Risk
The risk inherent to the entire market or entire market segment. Also known as "un-diversifiable risk" or "market risk." interest rates, recession and wars all represent sources of systematic risk because they will affect the entire market and cannot be avoided through

diversification. Whereas this type of risk affects a broad range of securities, unsystematic risk affects a very specific group of securities or an individual security. Systematic risk can be mitigated only by being hedged.

Systemic Risk
Risk that threatens an entire financial system.

S&P500
Standard & Poor's Index of the New York Stock Exchange. A basket of 500 stocks that are considered to be widely held. The S&P 500 index is weighted by market value, and its performance is thought to be representative of the stock market as a whole.

T

Treasury Bill
A negotiable debt obligation issued by the U.S. government and backed by its full faith and credit, having a maturity of one year or less. Exempt from state and local taxes. Also called Bill or T-Bill or U.S. Treasury Bill.

Time Value
The amount by which an option's premium exceeds its intrinsic value. Also called time premium.

Top-Down Investing
An investment strategy which first finds the best sectors or industries to invest in, and then searches for the best companies within those sectors or industries. This investing strategy begins with a look at the overall economic picture and then narrows it down to sectors, industries and companies that are expected to perform well. Analysis of the fundamentals of a given security is the final step.

Tracking Error
This statistic measures the standard deviation of a fund's excess returns over the returns of an index or benchmark portfolio. As such, it can be an indication of 'riskiness' in the manager's investment style. A Tracking Error below 2 suggests a passive approach, with a close

fit between the fund and its benchmark. At 3 and above the correlation is progressively looser: the manager will be deploying a more active investment style, and taking bigger positions away from the benchmark's composition.

Traded Endowment Policy - TEP

An Endowment Policy is a type of life insurance that has a value that is payable to the insured if he/she is still living on the policy's maturity date, or to a beneficiary otherwise. They are normally "with profits policies". If the insured does not wish to wait until maturity to receive the value they can either surrender it back to the issuing insurance company, or they can sell the policy on the open market. If the policy is sold it then becomes a Traded Endowment Policy or TEP. TEP Funds aim to buy and sell TEPs at advantageous prices to make a profit.

Traded Options

Transferable options with the right to buy or sell a standardised amount of a security at a fixed price within a specified period.

Traditional Investments

Includes equities, bonds, high yield bonds, emerging markets debt, cash, cash equivalents.

U

Umbrella Fund

An investment company which has a group of sub-funds (pools) each having its own investment portfolio. The purpose of this structure is to provide investment flexibility and widen investor choice.

Underlier or Underlying Security

A security or commodity, which is subject to delivery upon exercise of an option contract or convertible security. Exceptions include index options and futures, which cannot be delivered and are therefore settled in cash.

Underweight

A situation where a portfolio does not hold a sufficient amount of securities to satisfy the accepted benchmark of the portfolio's asset allocation strategy. For example, if a portfolio normally holds 40% stock and currently holds 30%, the position in equities would be considered underweight.

Unit Trust

A common form of collective investment (similar to a mutual fund) where investors' money is pooled and invested into a variety of shares and bonds in order to reduce risk. Its capital structure is open ended as units can be created or redeemed depending on demand from investors. It should be noted that a Unit Trust means something completely different in the US.

V

Value of New Business VNB

Sum of all income (i.e. charges) from new policies minus costs of setting up the policies (i.e. commission) discounted to present day value.

Value Stocks

Stocks which are perceived to be selling at a discount to their intrinsic or potential worth, i.e. undervalued; or stocks which are out of favour with the market and are under-followed by analysts. It is believed that the share price of these stocks will increase as the value of the company is recognised by the market.

Value-Added Monthly Index (VAMI)

An index that tracks the monthly performance of a hypothetical $1000 investment. The calculation for the current month's VAMI is: Previous VAMI x (1 + Current Rate of Return)

The value-added monthly index charts the total return gained by an investor from reinvestment of any dividends and additional interest gained through compounding. The VAMI index is sometimes used to evaluate the performance of a fund manager.

Venture Capital

Money and resources made available to start-up firms and small businesses with exceptional growth potential. Venture capital often also includes managerial and technical expertise. Most venture capital money comes from an organized group of wealthy investors who seek substantially above average returns and who are willing to accept correspondingly high risks. This form of raising capital is increasingly popular among new companies that, because of a limited operating history, can't raise money through a debt issue. The downside for entrepreneurs is that venture capitalists usually receive a say in the major decisions of the company in addition to a portion of the equity.

Volatility

Standard deviation is a statistical measurement which, when applied to an investment fund, expresses its volatility, or risk. It shows how widely a range of returns varied from the fund's average return over a particular period. Low volatility reduces the risk of buying into an investment in the upper range of its deviation cycle, then seeing its value head towards the lower extreme. For example, if a fund had an average return of 5%, and its volatility was 15, this would mean that the range of its returns over the period had swung between +20% and -10%. Another fund with the same average return and 5% volatility would return between 10% and nothing, but there would at least be no loss.

Printed in Great Britain
by Amazon